I AM—I CAN

I AM
I CAN

Daniel C. Steere

FLEMING H. REVELL COMPANY

OLD TAPPAN, NEW JERSEY

All Scripture quotations in this volume are from the Revised Standard Version of the Bible, copyrighted 1946 and 1952, and used by permission.

Library of Congress Cataloging in Publication Data

Steere, Daniel C
     I am—I can.

     1. Christian life—Methodist authors.
2. Success. I. Title.
BV4501.2.S753   248'.48'76   73–6921
ISBN 0–8007–0618–8

TO
Norma

Contents

I do not want merely to possess a faith;
I want a faith that possesses me.

—Charles Kingsley

I AM—I CAN

1 To Possess a Faith That Possesses Me!

You are using less than 10 percent of your potential!

If you are like most people, you probably believe the person you are now is pretty well the total you. You couldn't be more wrong. A vast depth of power, talent, and ability lies within you. In fact, to think about the *amount* of potential within you is utterly staggering.

Competent people, talented people, dynamic people possess no more ability than you do—they are just using more of their potential than you are. Everything there is about you now is just a tiny fraction of who you can be once you understand how to tap the great reservoir of talent and ability which lies unused within you.

Think about this: If you could tap just 10 percent more of the inner abilities you have, you would be *twice* the person you are now!

I read in a newspaper recently an Associated Press story about a woman in Kentucky who pulled a two-thousand-pound car off her little son after they had plunged into a

ditch. "He was pinned under the car," she said, "and I
didn't even think about how heavy the car was. I knew
I had to get it off him, so I did."

In an emergency a person will sometimes respond instinctively and summon up tremendous strength of body
or character. Later when he thinks back on the episode, he
may be dumbfounded that he possessed such physical
strength, courage, or cool-headedness. We know there are
vast reserves of potential within people. The problem has
been to find a way of harnessing those reserves so that we
can use them in everyday life.

Now through the contributions of doctors, psychologists,
ministers, and many others, we can put the pieces of the
puzzle together with considerable clarity and insight. A
concept called "Power-Faith" will be discussed in this
book. *Power-Faith* is a technique for putting it all together.

Faith is the most powerful force in the universe! God
is certainly the source of power, so I am speaking of the
force of that power and not the *source*. Faith allows God's
power to move and work in your life. The presence of
God's awesome power does you precious little good if you
do not allow that power to work in you.

In the ninth chapter of Matthew's Gospel, Jesus heals
four people in three episodes. A ruler came to Jesus as he
was teaching one day. He asked Jesus to come and visit
his daughter, who had just died.

As Jesus was on his way to the man's house, a woman
who had suffered from hemorrhaging for twelve years
came up behind and touched his robe, saying to herself:
"If I only touch his garment, I shall be made well." Jesus
turned to her and said: "Take heart, daughter; your faith
has made you well" (Matthew 9:21, 22).

Later, Jesus was approached by two blind men who asked for his mercy. Jesus touched their eyes and said to them: "According to your faith be it done to you. And their eyes were opened" (Matthew 9:29, 30).

In a related episode, St. Luke tells the beautiful story of Mary, the woman who washed Jesus' feet with her tears. After she had dried his feet with her hair and bathed them with ointment, Jesus said to her: "Your faith has saved you; go in peace" (Luke 7:50).

People have puzzled over Jesus' words in those stories for many years. The question is asked over and over: Why did Jesus say to these people that their *faith* had saved them, or made them well? Why did he not say: "God's power has saved you; God's power has made you well"? Jesus was not denying the work was God's; he was affirming the role faith plays in bringing God's power into action.

The tremendous power of faith can be the most exciting discovery you ever make. Why? Because faith is the key which opens before you all the infinite possibilities of life.

Power-Faith is a way of looking at life. It is a system for breaking life down into workable segments and mastering them one by one. If you will believe this system works, it can change your life. Power-Faith living can literally work a miracle in you.

There are three areas of living which you need to see in a new perspective: yourself, the design of life, and God's power to make you a whole person. You need to learn how to develop real Power-Faith by redirecting your thinking about these three areas of life. It will be an exciting journey if you will believe Power-Faith works.

You will learn how to have faith in yourself, how to believe in yourself. You will see that God has placed everything about life completely at your disposal. You will learn how to use life as your tool. Finally, you will understand how God's power can change your life.

There are six simple principles which outline Power-Faith living. They are basic truths about the three areas of life on which you can build your entire view of existence.

FAITH IN YOURSELF

1. Your self-image determines who you really are. Who you are will always be consistent with who you think you are.
2. You are using only a fraction of the potential within you.

FAITH IN LIFE

3. You must overcome your awe of life before you can master it.
4. Life was made for man, not man for life. You are fulfilling God's plan for you as you begin to master successful living.
5. Security must come from within. Security from outside can be taken away from you.

FAITH IN GOD'S POWER

6. God is designed into His plan for life. He is the greatest source of power you have.

If you will believe these principles are true, and apply them to your life, it will give you the mental attitude which can make your living produce positive results. As you will see, your mental attitude absolutely determines whether your actions will be productive in life.

Likewise your mental attitude determines whether God can be a part of your life. If you choose to face life by yourself, God will allow you to go it alone. He respects your freedom to decide your own spiritual destiny. If you will have faith that God is on your side, if you will allow God's power to make you whole, the difference will literally be that of *life* versus *no life.*

Six little principles about living can provide the outlook you need to make your life productive. Faith in these principles will give you a foundation on which to build a set of goals higher than you ever dreamed you could attain. It will give you a mental attitude which enables you to function with a competence and effectiveness you have never experienced.

Power-Faith is not a panacea which can dispel all of your worries. Neither is it a cure-all which will protect you from the hard knocks of life.

Power-Faith is a view of life which enables your own hard work to focus in an effective process of growth. It helps you develop a confident attitude toward yourself, toward life, and toward God's loving concern for you.

It is not a garment to wrap yourself in for protection. It is not a magic spell to shield you from failure. You have to do the work of accomplishing your goals. The fact is that your view of yourself, life, and God may have to be drastically changed before your behavior becomes effective on your behalf.

Power-Faith will do nothing for you if you only think about it. Faith must be lived. As you come to understand the difference between wishing and knowing, between thinking and doing, you will understand why faith has to be lived. Power-Faith living opens every horizon of possibility to you.

Developing self-confidence is a big step toward finding inner peace. Power-Faith is more than just a mental attitude. It is an attitude which allows you to begin living successfully.

Developing self-confidence and inner peace have become popular subjects in recent years. Many books have been written about improving self-confidence and approaching life positively. They are all fine books and are helpful as far as they go. Power-Faith, however, is a more comprehensive method of learning to manage life.

You have been led to believe by some people that all you need to do to overcome your doubts and fears is to improve your self-image. That is only partly true. Improving your self-image is only the first step in learning to manage life.

I believe it is a basic, beginning step, but self-image improvement alone is an inadequate foundation when you first venture to believe there is more for you in life.

As a second step, you must come to accept the fact that life is at your disposal. Life is given you so you may take advantage of it. Life is an exciting tool. But like any tool, you have to learn how to use it before it becomes very helpful.

And, third, you should understand how the power of God works in your life, and how it can add a dimension of such depth and scope as to transform you and your life almost miraculously.

We will begin by discussing self-image and move on to talk about how exciting it is to really live and take advantage of life, then about how the power of God adds to *your* power in managing life. By the time you have gone that far, life should seem much less overawing, and you will understand better that you have a great reservoir of power and talent within you.

It helps to keep the word *power* with the word *faith* because the two together express the exciting secret of tapping the limitless possibilities of life. In fact, faith is not fully developed until it *is* Power-Faith.

There is a difference in believing and in having faith, the Reverend Billy Graham has said, although in common usage the words tend to overlap. You can believe in something without having any faith in it. Many people believe in God without ever living a life of faith. Remember, the Book of James reminds us: "Even the demons believe—and shudder" (2:19). If you believe in something enough so that you have faith in it, then you make a commitment to that faith. It is one thing to believe a rocket can fly, but it becomes an act of faith when you commit your life to that belief by going aboard and letting that rocket blast off beneath you.

A famous aerialist was approaching the end of his career. He had accomplished almost every feat a high-wire artist could perform. The one remaining dream of his life was to walk a tightrope across Niagara Falls. Finally he was able to arrange it. The press played it up with great fanfare, and on the day of his performance great throngs had gathered on each side.

The aerialist took his long balancing pole and started out. The crowd gasped and exclaimed as he made his way slowly across the raging cataract. Finally he was across and a mighty roar went up from the crowd. The man beamed in triumph, then brought a small wheelbarrow out onto the platform. "I'm going to walk back across the falls," he called down, "wheeling a man in this wheelbarrow in front of me." A gasp went up. "Do you believe I can do it?" he called down.

"Yes!" shouted back the crowd.

The aerialist pointed to a man below him. "Do you believe I can do it?" The man nodded, grinned, and waved vigorously in encouragement.

"Okay, you're first," the aerialist replied—and the man fainted.

That's the difference between believing and having faith. It takes belief to accomplish faith. They go together, but faith begins with willingness to commit your life to whatever you believe in.

Believing in yourself must become *faith* in yourself. Believing in God must become *faith* in God. Believing in life must become *faith* that all of life is at your disposal.

Perhaps there is even a prior need. You probably don't believe there is much real power in faith. Before you can get excited about committing your life to these three things, you must believe there is a key that will unlock the universe, and that *faith* in these three *is* that key. Faith in yourself, in life, and in God's power is Power-Faith! Through Power-Faith all things are possible, just as God has told us.

Jesus said faith could move mountains, but you don't really believe that! If you did, you would be moving mountains. People who have faith in themselves can move the most awesome mountains you could imagine. If you are one who develops that faith, you will move mountains, also.

Psychologists tell us most people use only about 10 percent of their potential. About 90 percent of most people's abilities lie unused, and perhaps undiscovered, throughout all their lives.

The biggest problem psychologists and motivational experts face is in convincing people that who they are right now is just a tiny part of who they could be. Most people believe that whoever they are presently is all there ever could be to them. They believe the 10 percent or so is really 100 percent of them. Not so!

You can rest assured that everything there is about you now is only a tiny fraction of your potential. No matter who you are, or what you are, that is a fact about you—90 percent of you is lying undiscovered, undreamed of, deep within you.

The second problem is in convincing you that *faith* is the key to unleashing that other 90 percent of you. Faith is the source of fantastic, limitless power within you. That's why it is Power-Faith. That's why it is the key. Like God's power, your inner resources are already here, and Power-Faith is simply the unleashing of the potential that lies within you.

Let me illustrate this fact of your untapped potential with a story frequently employed by motivational experts. It is the most remarkable true story I have ever heard.

One of the great coaches of college football was Lou Little of Columbia University. One day, the University chancellor stopped Lou on campus and told him of the sudden death of the father of one of the boys who played football.

"I wish you would break the news to the boy," he said.

"I hear the boy and his dad were unusually close, and it might be easier coming from you."

Coach Little sought the boy out in the locker room, took him aside, and gently broke the news of his father's death. "I know how close the two of you were," Coach Little told him. "Take as much time off as you need. Don't worry about your studies or football practice. We all understand and will help you work it out when you return."

The boy left on Wednesday, and Friday afternoon was back on the practice field. Coach Little saw him and walked over. "Hello, son," he said. "What are you doing back so soon? You could have taken a week or two, helped your mother get things in order. We would have understood."

"Coach," the boy replied, "my father was buried yesterday, and the rest of the family is taking care of things. Coach Little, I've just got to play in that game tomorrow. That's why I came back today."

Now that posed a problem for the coach. "You know, tomorrow's game will be the most important game of the season," he reminded the boy. "If we win tomorrow, we will win the conference championship; if we lose tomorrow, we lose the championship. You aren't a usual starter, son, and there's a good chance you might not play at all."

The boy nodded, "I know I haven't played much, Coach, but I'm asking you for a chance to play tomorrow. I've just got to play in that game."

Coach Little thought for a minute and said: "Okay, son, tell you what. If we win the toss, I'll let you play on the receiving team, but I can't promise you more than that."

The day of the game Columbia won the toss, and Coach

Little sent the boy in to receive the kick. He not only caught the ball; he ripped back up the field laying out opponents left and right. He almost scored a touchdown. So the coach left him in. During the course of the game, he played both offense and defense like a demon. He ran, caught passes, blocked, tackled, and scored three touchdowns. He was fantastic, and largely because of his play, they won the game. When the game was over, Coach Little sought out the boy in the locker room.

"What in the world happened to you out there?" he asked. "You never played ball like that in your whole life. That's the best exhibition of football I ever saw. How in the world did you do it?"

"Well, Coach," the boy said, "you never met my father, did you?"

"No, I didn't," replied Coach Little. "I knew you were very close to your father, and I saw you walking arm in arm across the campus on several occasions, but I never met him."

"Well, you see," the boy began, and paused, searching for words, "for most of my life my father was blind—and today was the first day he was able to watch me play."

Faith changed that young man! It unleashed great abilities which had lain dormant until then because the boy did not have faith that they were there. That true story is very real proof that there is tremendous power in faith. There is enough power in faith to transform any ordinary, mediocre person into a person of great ability. If you only knew of the untapped resources you have! The first hurdle is to convince yourself that everything there is to you is only a fraction of who you can be. When you have no doubt that there is an almost limitless potential within you, then you are ready for the second step, which is trying to tap that potential.

Do not try to jump to the second step without coping with the first, however, or you will fail, and create serious obstacles. If you only *wish* there were great physical, or emotional, or creative resources within you, if you only desperately try to convince yourself, you will not find them there when you take that leap of faith. You will fail, and that failure will just convince you of your mediocrity.

Power-Faith grows out of your firm conviction that your unused resources do exist. You have to know it, believe it, be convinced of it. You must feel it as a definite reality about you, with a quiet, humble confidence that will remain unshaken no matter what might cause you to doubt yourself. Once something shakes your faith, you will rapidly plunge back into your old mediocre image of yourself and be even more afraid to try again, because your feelings of mediocrity or inadequacy are more firmly implanted than before.

Begin your change by thinking seriously about the possibility that there is more to you than you ever saw before. There is, and you must become used to thinking of yourself as a gross underachiever. Almost everyone in the world is in the same position. You can be a 15 percent utilizer and be above average. That's right. The average is so pitifully low that it is no compliment to be called average. Anyone with any drive at all can be above average. Almost all mediocre people are average because they allow themselves to be, and not because they are limited for life by inferior talents and inferior minds. To be sure, there are some people who are mentally retarded and have very limited capacity for accomplishment. There are some who are mentally ill and medical science has not found a way to cure their malady. If you can read and understand the statements about Power-Faith, you are probably not locked into either of these categories. The most probable cause of your underachieving, or of your being a very average person, is that you are convinced that this is all there is to you.

Suppose you could be convinced that most of your potential lies, like an iceberg, buried within you. Suppose you could change your image of yourself and have supreme confidence that by utilizing more of your potential you could become a dynamic and positive-oriented person, capable of accomplishing almost anything you tackled.

That is the first step: getting past the point of saying, "Suppose I am more," and reaching the point of saying: "Yes, I am more!"

2 We Have Met the Enemy and He Is Us!

This take-off on Admiral Perry's familiar statement is almost as famous as the original. It has become popular because it strikes at a fundamental truth about people. Too often we are our own worst enemy.

A down-and-out derelict stood on a street corner one day and watched a big limousine bearing a boyhood friend drive by. With a philosophical shrug he sighed: "Ah, there but for me, go I."

You may well be your own worst enemy because you do not have faith in yourself.

A young woman called one day and said she had a terrible problem. When we sat down to talk, she began to cry, and through her sobs poured out a story of a courtship and engagement filled with fighting, unhappiness, and physical violence at the hands of the girl's fiancé. "I realize he is taking advantage of me and misusing me," she confessed, "but I feel like I might not find another man to marry if I lose him."

"Why do you believe that?" I asked her.

"Because," she replied, "I'm not very attractive, I just can't seem to make decisions on my own, and I don't have very much self-confidence. I don't do most things very well, and I usually mess up anything I begin. I'm just not the kind of girl most men are looking for."

Now I am a firm believer in the truth of this statement: *Who you are will always be consistent with who you think you are!*

That's the premise on which I base much of my counseling.

We talked for a long while that morning. We talked about her lack of confidence in herself, about her feelings that life is too big, and she too inadequate to really take advantage of much of it. We discussed the power of God to work in the world, and how God's power works in people.

We were talking Power-Faith, although I hadn't begun to call it that at the time.

We began to discuss the possibility of untapped potential within this young woman. I talked with her about the need to see herself as an underachiever. We discussed the possibility that her insecure and erratic behavior might indeed grow out of her belief that she was in total only an inadequate, mediocre person. She had never considered that she might be blocking out reserves of strength and energy because of an inadequate picture of herself. She did not like who she was, but felt powerless to become anything more. As a result, she was calling forth very small quantities of her true resources.

We talked together over a period of several months. During that time, the young woman struggled to understand what these new concepts of herself and of God's power to work through her might mean. She eventually found the strength to call off her ill-fated engagement. Soon she began to exhibit signs of new interest in life, new enthusiasm. Her visits became fewer and more widely spaced. It took some months for her to absorb the totality of Power-Faith thinking, but in time it changed her life. The young lady is now married quite happily, to a much more mature and stable man, and has more confidence and verve for life than any three people usually do. I wish you could see her smile as she begins to talk about how much she is enjoying life now that she feels it is manageable, and about her self-assurance, which is quite remarkable.

During that long period of struggling to overcome her self-doubts, she began to pray with real earnestness for the first time in her life. Since she was not a very religious person by upbringing, she did not know how to pray formally, so she talked with God in her own fashion, mostly in simple conversations. Sometimes she talked out loud, sometimes silently. She asked for strength. She asked for understanding. She asked for God's peace within.

God responded to her in that time of need. She was given strength, and understanding, and eventually, calmness and peace within her soul.

Power-Faith works! Power-Faith proves itself over and over as one after another discovers how it changes lives.

I will never forget how surprised I was to discover that the prettiest girl in high school had a severe inferiority complex. She was to my mind an ideal person—sweet, sincere, and very unassuming. Because of those qualities, she was a favorite of everyone, boys and girls alike. People felt good being with her, and her friends held a genuine love for her. Yet she suffered from serious feelings of inadequacy and inferiority. "How could that be?" I wondered. "She has everything a person should need to be happy."

Her problem was that she didn't believe in herself. Even though other people saw her as a wonderful person, she had a different view.

Many people are like that. If you don't allow yourself to believe what you see, you can be blind to your own strengths and positive assets. Remember—the brain interprets what the eye sees, and it is always the *interpreted* meaning of reality which becomes our view of what is real or true.

We become our own worst enemy when we decide we are not capable of coping with life, or that many of life's opportunities are beyond our reasonable expectations because we are average, below average, unattractive, a failure, or a million other reasons.

Someone told me a story about pike, which are a type of fish. According to the story, pike may be placed in a tank with a glass partition down the middle and minnows put on the other side. The pike, who love to eat minnows, will begin a desperate attempt to get to the minnows, butting against the glass fruitlessly for some time. Finally they will give up and quit trying.

The glass partition may then be removed. The pike will be free to eat the minnows, but a strange thing will have happened. The pike have gotten it into their heads that the minnows are not available for food. They will swim around among those little fish, hungry as ever, but believing still that the minnows are not available.

If that story is true, it is a remarkable description of some people I know.

Once some folks have decided that something in life is not available, they will go through their whole lives accepting that decision as a foregone conclusion.

They might begin preparing themselves for overcoming the problem, or watching for the right opportunity to come along, but do not because they have already decided the "truth" about themselves and "know" they could not really attain that lofty goal.

There are two important steps in reaching lofty goals:

First, be open to growth. Let your weaker points be friendly signals that you need to grow in some area.

Second and just as importantly, you must take advantage of opportunities in life. Make good things happen by trying every door you can find. If you try enough doors, one will open somewhere along the way.

It takes both steps to attain goals you desire. We are now talking about step one. It may not seem as exciting as learning to get out and make life happen, but it is exciting when you become a positive-oriented, growing person with confidence and personal faith. When you are growing and believing, you are setting the stage for your ability to take opportunities and do something great with them.

When you decide that lofty goals are not attainable because of inadequacies or shortcomings, you stifle and confine your mind. That view of yourself becomes a straightjacket which keeps you from growing into a new person who *is* capable of attaining exciting goals.

You become like those pike. Opportunities present themselves, but you ignore them. Perhaps you don't even notice them as opportunities, because you have decided it takes someone else with much more to offer to make something of life's great opportunities.

That makes you your own worst enemy. Nobody else has to work against you. You have determined your own future, and it is a very sad one.

There is another type of mental block. It is entirely possible to form barriers you are not aware of.

Imagine you allowed yourself to be hypnotized by a person you trusted. Then suppose the hypnotist drew a line across the floor and said to you: "You will not be able to cross this line no matter how hard you try." After instilling that command in your mind, he could also cause you to forget that you had been hypnotized, then wake you.

That line the hypnotist drew would become as real a barrier as if it were a solid wall. Unaware you had been hypnotized, you might attempt to cross the room for something without thinking about it. On approaching the imaginary line, you would hesitate, stop dead, and have to make a choice. You would either change your mind and decide you didn't really want to cross the room after all, or you would be thrown into a quandary because you could not proceed.

Try as you might, you could not cross that line. Since you would not consciously know you had been left with a posthypnotic suggestion, your mind might have to invent some reason for your not crossing the line. Changing your mind would be one of those alternatives. You might stumble, or develop a terrible fear of going into the other part of the room, or you could very well just stand at the line, confused and perplexed.

Does that situation sound like any you have encountered in real life? It should; people live in a world of psychological barriers.

Having fun at parties or social gatherings may be a real mental block to you because of your own feelings of insecurity, self-consciousness, or whatever. You may rationalize your poor self-image instead of admitting it to yourself, though. "I don't like parties, they are loud and boring." "Most people are a drag." "I'm too tired to go anywhere tonight." "I'm not in the mood." Those excuses, if they occur often, may signal that you have a psychological barrier concerning social relationships.

Your hang-up may be feelings of inadequacy when you are in groups. It might be a fear of competing with other people. People who spend their whole lives using one excuse after another to avoid social relationships are functioning as their own worst enemies.

It might be most helpful if you could make a list of your biggest hang-ups. What are your psychological barriers? Everyone has some. Nothing can equal the joy and thrill of overcoming a psychological barrier that has really bothered you.

School is that mental barrier to some people. They often do not realize they have that attitude toward school. They have made up all sorts of excuses about why they cannot finish school, or pass a subject, or raise their grades, or go back for that graduate work they dream of so often.

A negative self-image can literally cause your mind to draw lines over which you cannot cross. When all the excuses are stripped away, you are likely to find that a failure in your life, or an unfilled dream, was really caused by a psychological barrier of which you were not aware.

A popular song talks of a man who drifted from one dream to another. He was seeking that one break, that one place where he would find happiness and security. The song tells of his love for his wife who followed him from place to place, of the loss of a child, and of his sorrow that he could not give his wife much to show for their rootless life. "We went to Birmingham," he sings, "and a gold mine in Alaska." They didn't find it in Birmingham, or the gold mine in Alaska, or anywhere else they went.

That song echoes the fruitless search for success and happiness made by so many people. It illustrates the same point I have been talking about.

The mind is controlled by your self-image. If success or happiness constantly eludes you, if every venture you try fails, you are almost certainly the reason for your failure. If success is on the other side of a psychological barrier like the hypnotist's line, you will not be able to cross it. You will do something that causes you to fail. You will make a bad decision, invest your money foolishly, handle things poorly, give up too soon, or perhaps even get sick. If you are not aware of the real reason for your failure, you may be ready to try something else soon after. "Just wait, I've really got it this time. You'll see!"

Think about the illustration of the hypnotist and the imaginary line. Psychological barriers like that occur in real life all the time. They are caused by poor self-image. They are as real as prison walls or chasms. You are usually not aware of those barriers, but you can become aware of them. The key to erasing them is to become conscious of them, then honestly believe you can cross them. The words *joy* and *thrill* are inadequate to describe the feeling of crossing a former psychological barrier. It is the most wonderful feeling you can imagine!

The real truth about you is that you can do almost anything you want to, but you must believe you can. The strength and capacity to cope with life are within you. The ability to attain lofty goals is within you. If you are operating as an inadequate person, it is because you have formed this inadequate mental picture of yourself, or are not aware of subconscious mental barriers and have straightjacketed your abilities.

It is not just the situations of life that affect you. How you interpret your function in those situations is just as important. You may be displeased with your performance in a situation when no one else noticed anything particularly lacking in your behavior. You may feel yourself more inadequate than you really are.

You may sit in a corner feeling inadequate when, if you put away your self-pity and moodiness and joined in a group with a smile, no one would ever have a thought about your being inadequate. Others usually have no idea anyone might be inadequate until they catch signs that the person feels himself to be inadequate.

People are usually harder on themselves than others are. Sometimes a person will do something wrong. His friends will forgive him, God will forgive him, but he cannot forgive himself.

That person may be unable to accept the forgiveness of his friends, or of God, because he is still blaming himself. Until he is able to forgive himself, he may not be able to really *believe* his friends, and God, have forgiven him.

People may develop the same fault in being overly critical of themselves. It is easy to believe that everyone is very aware of your mistakes and shortcomings. You may refuse to believe you are normal and adequate because you are self-conscious about every error and failure.

It can become a very negative viewpoint if you are too critical of yourself. Self-criticism should be levelheaded, and oriented to the positive.

Criticism is positive when it leads to healthy growth. It is negative when it becomes a defeatist "I can't do it" attitude.

Remember, it is positively true that you possess more power and strength within you than you could ever use fully. If you are not satisfied with your performance in coping with emotions, pressure, responsibility, or whatever, let it be a signal for you to begin reaching within for a little of the untapped ability which is lying there waiting to be used.

Begin the following things in this order:

Begin to grow.
Expect to grow slowly.
Practice whenever you can.
Develop as positive an attitude toward yourself as you can.
Believe in yourself as you grow.

As you watch yourself grow slowly, you will begin to develop faith in your ability to function more strongly. Don't rush things, but do expect to grow steadily. Remember that you are still only tapping a tiny portion of the power within you.

As your faith in yourself increases, it will release more

and more of that great power to you. Only your imagination limits you as you grow.

When you were blocking out your inner powers to function in life, you were your own worst enemy. When you begin releasing that vast reservoir of power and talent, you become your own greatest asset. Nothing is outside the scope of your growth. If you can dream it, you can attain it.

3 Self-Image

Psychologists have learned that a person's self-image (who you see yourself to be) is the most important factor in determining who you really are. You literally become in real life just the kind of person your mind tells you that you are.

Dr. Maxwell Maltz, in his book, *Psycho-Cybernetics*, explores in much greater detail than we shall, the reasons for the computer-like qualities of the human mind. Rest assured, though, that the greatest computers man can design are clumsy imitations of the human brain. The principles on which computers operate are taken from the way man himself functions.

The old idea about self-image was that it served as a mirror, reflecting who a person is. The idea of self-image is changing. Now many psychologists and counselors are convinced that a person's self-image *determines* who he is, rather than merely reflecting who he is. The reason that

39

is true is that the human mind operates just like a computer.

Man's brain stores up all sorts of facts, experiences, feelings, emotions, and we call it *learning*, or *knowledge*. Like a computer, the mind can give back only something which has been placed in its memory mechanism. When you program a computer, it will play back exactly what you have told it to do, no more, and no less. The computer may be large enough to perform the most complicated tasks, using integral calculus, geometry, algebra, and so on. But if your program for it limits the machine to adding and subtracting simple numbers, all the vast capacity within the computer is wasted.

Your self-image is the "program" which sets the limits and functions for you to operate as a person. If you tell your mind you are a very average, or inadequate person, you are literally locking your mind into that sort of behavior. Like a computer, your mind *must* obey the instructions you give it. Your self-image is that set of instructions.

A company in my city owns a computer so large they have never tested its ultimate capacity. On that huge computer the company has solved complicated problems relating to outer space. They have plotted and predicted all the factors which must be known in order to send a rocket into space, and bring it back. The computer is so large that companies all across the nation rent time and space on it. Companies in cities several thousand miles away can be connected to the computer by telephone line, and answers to complicated problems, or long lists of statistics and tabulations, can be fed back to the distant city instantly.

Imagine feeding a program into that vast computer

which would limit it to performing as nothing more than a common adding machine!

You are doing that to your mind if you are living with a negative self-image.

Everything you know to be good or bad, right or wrong, true or false, has been taught you. That information is stored away in your mind and becomes part of the knowledge you use to make decisions and judgments. Just as a computer works with all its information to come up with an answer, your brain sorts through all its information and puts together its decisions.

Now, the reason it is important to know this about your brain is that this is how your self-image is formed. Poor self-image really grows out of a vicious cycle which develops as you grow through childhood.

When you do something well or poorly, your mind takes note of it. Soon you begin making value judgments about yourself. You say: "I'm just terrible at arithmetic," or, "I am very good at baseball." You decide on the basis of a social fluff or embarrassment that you are socially unattractive, or do not relate well to the opposite sex. An image of who you are begins forming.

Now you probably knew that already. What you may not know is that there is a second and more important consequence. The mind does not make these judgments about who you are just so you can be aware of yourself. *The mind makes these judgments about who you are so it will know how to make you act!*

Your mind controls who you are!

If you believe you are a very mediocre person, your mind causes you to *act* very mediocre, and that vicious cycle takes hold. When you do something poorly, you say

to yourself, "Aha, I was right; I am a very stupid person.
I knew it all along." The more firmly your mind believes
that image of you, the more consistently it will cause you
to act out mediocrity in all those areas of life where you
feel yourself to be average or inadequate.

Some people have an even worse self-image. They see
themselves as failures. If you believe you are a failure,
your mind is duty bound by that self-image to make you
act like a failure.

*Who you are will always be consistent with who you
think you are!*

It has not been very long since psychiatrists discovered
that your self-image is not the permanent truth about you.
You can change your image of yourself.

You cannot be a successful person, or a dynamic, creative person, or even a happy person, if you believe yourself to be unsuccessful, or mediocre, or inadequate. But on
the other hand, if you *know* you are a person with talent,
or ability, or capacity for success, if you have real faith in
yourself as an adequate, capable person, then you will begin being that new person. It has to be real faith, though.

The great breakthrough in developing faith in yourself
will come when you can honestly accept things such as
failure, inadequacy, or mediocrity as being only a tempo-
rary truth about you. This amazing human brain causes
any of those attributes to be the truth about you, as long
as you believe it. Believe you are inadequate, and you will
be inadequate; believe you are capable, and you *will be!*

Of course, the burning question is: "How do I stop feeling inferior, or inadequate, or a failure? It may be easy for
someone else to reevaluate himself if he has talents and
abilities, but I'm just plain, inadequate, average me. I

can't change much because I don't have very much to work with."

Begin right here with your belief that there isn't much of you to work with. It just is not true. God has created you with unbelievable capacities and abilities. You are simply not using most of them.

The first step in changing who you are is getting used to thinking of yourself as an underachiever. Begin seeing yourself as one who, like most people, is not using most of his potential. Begin understanding that many people have discovered inner resources and are using them.

Pick out someone you admire, someone who has some qualities or talents you would like to have. Begin now thinking of both you and that person as being equal in every way *in potential*. I am not saying you will have the same talents. But everyone has a great many talents and much more capability than he has ever used. You have great reserves of talent and capability which you have never touched.

You are an underachiever. You have restricted your ability to function by programming your mind with a limiting, maybe even a crippling, self-image. There is more to you. Say it to yourself. Believe it. When you honestly believe it, the time will come when you can put your faith in it. When that happens, when you can put your faith in the fact that you are an underachiever with undiscovered reserves of potential, you will begin to act differently.

Faith precedes tapping your potential. Faith is the key which unlocks it. Once you develop genuine faith that more of you is within, you are able to begin using your inner resources. You will begin drawing upon your unused depth.

Potential is most valuable when you put it to work and it becomes reality. It can be valuable in another way, though. If you have faith that there is more beyond your present capacities, it can give you great confidence as you move through everyday life.

There is a difference between seeing who you are now as being all there is to you, and believing you are only using a tiny fraction of all that is within you!

A man I know struggled with the most serious self-doubts for many years. It was evident to people who knew him that even though he was a nice guy, and seemed to have everything a man would need to be successful, he lacked self-confidence. His self-doubts ate away at him so relentlessly that he became less and less able to function as a man, a company executive, or even a husband.

Finally, a perceptive marriage counselor offered a piece of advice which began immediately to break the vicious cycle of poor image—causing poor performance—causing poorer image, etc.

The counselor suggested to this friend's wife that she could help a great deal by changing her relationship with her husband.

"You have told me of your husband's increasing dependence on you, almost as if you were becoming his mother. You have told me how irritating his lack of initiative is, and how much it bothers you when you have to make decisions you feel he should make.

"Take a new look at your influence on your husband. Because you are frustrated, you nag, and gripe, and complain. You are helping to reinforce his self-doubts. Instead, find every opportunity to brag about things he does. Tell him how much he means to you, and how much you need him. Convince him that you really do need him. Convince him that you really do think he is wonderful. If he feels he is the doormat of the world, let him at least be appreciated at home!"

The friend's wife saw her attitudes toward her husband in a new light. She did love him, and wanted to see her husband lose his self-doubts. She did believe his doubts were unfounded.

She began to change her relationship with him. It was not an overnight formula, but the process of a couple of years. It worked like nothing you ever saw before. This self-doubting friend began to understand that his wife respected him, she adored him, she needed him. As he became convinced of these things, he began to *be* these things, just a little more at first, but to an ever greater extent as time went by. Before very long, his confidence in himself at home as someone who was needed and depended on began to spill over into other areas of life. Today my friend is a different person. His self-doubts have faded into the background and he is happy, successful, and productive. He believes in himself again.

You might want to consult a competent counselor of some kind if you really find it impossible to get past your self-doubts. It is not an admission of failure to talk with a good counselor. It can be a stimulating and enlightening experience.

God also needs to be a part of any decision you make. He *wants* to be a part of your life, and will make available to you the great infinite powers of His creativity and strength. There is power in prayer because God hears and answers prayer.

The wife of my self-doubting friend told several of us

at a small gathering once: "As far as I'm concerned, prayer is the most wonderful discovery I have ever made. God worked through both of us during that long struggle. We could not have made it without Him."

If you are not used to including prayer in your search for solutions, you may not think it is very important. You may be too embarrassed to pray, or feel hypocritical after being only mildly religious most of your life.

That is because you don't have faith that prayer really works. You may not believe God really cares about you, or that God is at work in the world.

Remember that Power-Faith is more than just having faith in yourself. There may be great untapped potential within you, but God has more power than you will ever have. His limitless power is yours, also.

Remember the old saying, "The best place to find a helping hand is at the end of your wrist"? God's power works most often through you when it can enhance your own abilities and capacities.

How much do you have to work with? Ninety percent more of you than you have ever seen—and the limitless power of God!

4 Life Is at Your Disposal!

Peace of mind often rests upon a person's feeling secure and at ease with life. So many people feel ill at ease in the world, though. It seems awfully big sometimes. Life can be very overpowering and frightening.

It is not enjoyable when life is your enemy. The world can get very hostile at times. It is in those times, when life is most difficult, that Power-Faith becomes a valuable asset. Everyone can have faith in themselves and in God during easy times. It is when life becomes hard and frightening that real faith is put to the test.

If you can stand in the face of great difficulty or uncertainty with faith in yourself and in God's power to work through you, then your faith becomes a tool of the greatest value, because you can literally bet your life on it!

Money is not the key to life. At least, money alone is no key to managing life. Many people with money squander it because they lack the self-confidence or stability to use their money wisely.

Perhaps they cannot stand the pressures of business or finance. Maybe they feel inadequate to design and manage long-range plans. They might lack self-discipline or be easily swayed into bad judgments. As a result, many people squander money on fly-by-night ventures or get-rich-quick schemes. They gamble on risky deals or skirt the law for easy profits. A great deal of money is squandered away every year. Sometimes these lessons are paid for with a very high price.

Again, money is no key to managing life if the problem is unhappiness. Money cannot conquer unhappiness all by itself. How many times have you read in the paper about wealthy people who become so despondent and depressed they commit suicide, or have nervous breakdowns, or live miserable and unhappy lives?

Paul Simon, who with his partner Art Garfunkle recorded such beautiful songs as "Bridge Over Troubled Water," also wrote a poignant song about a rich man named Richard Cory. The plaintive story describes Mr. Cory through the envious eyes of one of his factory workers.

Richard Cory's picture is constantly in the papers, showing his appearance at the opera or entertaining on his yacht. He is influential in his political party and has everything this factory worker would like to have. "But," sings the man, "I work in his factory, and I curse the life I'm living, and I curse my poverty, and I wish that I could be Richard Cory."

The song concludes with a twist, though. One evening the factory worker is startled to read in his newspaper that Richard Cory has taken his life. "Why would he do that?" he must have been thinking. "I could have enjoyed

Richard Cory's life and been only too grateful for it. How could the man be unhappy when he had everything money can buy?"

Self-image contributes more to happiness in life than money does! Make no mistake, nothing outside yourself—money, prestige, popularity, fame—can make up for a lack of self-esteem. People with all those desperately sought accomplishments commit suicide every year.

The one thing which makes any or all of those attributes worth something is a strong, positive self-image. Money plus self-assurance is a true asset. Fame plus self-assurance is an asset. Outward circumstances can never bring happiness to one who has a negative self-image.

If you are desiring any of these accomplishments because you hope they might bring you the security and happiness you don't have now, you are kidding yourself.

Wise men have warned against spending life searching for fame and fortune for very good reasons, not just because they felt it was more appropriate for people to be unworldly. Every culture has sooner or later included in its heritage of commonsense wisdom some warning that too much obsession with money or prestige will destroy a person, or result in an unhappy life.

The reason is that life plays a cruel joke on those who seek after fame and fortune. The glitter and glamour of wealth and fame mislead many people into thinking they are the key to happiness because they control the circumstances of life around a person. Money and prestige seem to become artificial tools which can create happy circumstances and an ideal world by managing one's environment. The further one plunges down that road, the more futile the struggle becomes. An inadequate person will be frightened of life and unable to function adequately and competently no matter how opulent the surroundings or how well-known his name. In fact, part of the cruel joke is that wealth and fame frequently add great pressures that push a weak person over the brink to a breakdown, alcoholism, or even suicide.

All that is so unnecessary! Life is very manageable. It is intended to be. Life is exciting, and positive, and rewarding.

Life is the most marvelous tool God has created for you. Everything on earth has been put here at man's disposal. God intends for you to use life. He wants you to take advantage of all the things He has put here, and to use them as resources and opportunities.

In the first three chapters, we discussed two crucial concepts for improving self-confidence. The first is: *Who you are will always be consistent with who you think you are*. The second is that *you are an underachiever! There are enough buried reserves of capability and talent for you to be anyone you want to be*.

Add to those basic concepts of yourself a third basic truth. This fact is about life:

Most people have to overcome their awe of life before they can master it!

You need to understand exactly what that means, and why it is crucial to making opportunity work for you.

A myth is a fable or story which presents a legendary explanation of life, or a story about legendary persons. There are mythological stories about all sorts of supernatural beings, monsters, and happenings. There are myths about why it thunders, about how the earth was made, about why the rose has thorns, and so on.

If we can use this same word *myth* in a little different sense, to talk about life, it may be helpful.

It is a myth that life is too big to comprehend and too vast for you to understand. The idea of life's overwhelming nature is one of the concepts of life left over from childhood. Almost everyone has to overcome that awe of life as a part of maturing into adulthood. The trouble is that many people never quite shake the feeling deep down that life is too vast and complicated for them to ever understand it, much less for them to master it.

This may be particularly true of things which really awed and impressed you as a child. Children tend to accept the world as a great mystical universe completely beyond their comprehension. They cannot really conceive of lands beyond the horizon, nor can they comprehend the workings of a hospital, or a television station. The huge skyscrapers in the city are awe-inspiring monuments to men with superhuman powers who must have constructed them. In fact, all of life seems beyond understanding, except the little corner the child occupies. Stories of magical dragons and fairly-tale kingdoms seem as believable as the staggering sights of the real world.

Often these childhood attitudes toward life are carried over into adulthood. Doctors still overawe, freeways are a marvel, tall buildings are a wonder, and television, movies, or the printed word carry great authority.

Life seems, indeed, to be a sort of ongoing cosmic order in which you occupy a very insignificant space. People who can master the great life forces, and feel at ease moving in the stratosphere of design and decision making, still seem almost superhuman. "I could never be a doctor," you may have told yourself. "Doctors are much more outstanding people than I am." You may be overawed by successful politicians, architects, athletes, scientists, or wealthy people.

"There wouldn't be any use at all for me to try to become a college graduate, professional person, or a creative person," you say to yourself. "I could never do what those other people have done." So you settle for a rather unrewarding and ordinary existence and try to adjust within your limits as best you can.

Some people are perfectly happy to live simple lives, uncluttered with much creativity, decision making, or a need to grow and accomplish. They do not need this re-evaluation of life. But if a simple life with a minimum of growth, excitement, or creativity leaves you unfulfilled, you may wish desperately you knew how to break out of your dull existence.

There is nothing wrong with a simple, comfortable, non-growing life. There are not really very many people who prefer that life, though. Many people find it comfortable to settle for plain, mediocre lives because the world scares them, or because they feel inadequate to venture forth to anything bigger. They make peace with their little existences and resign themselves to their lives as gracefully as they can. They feel they have no real choice, and accept the "reality" that they are limited persons in limited lives.

You can be just as much at peace, just as comfortable, and a great deal more satisfied with your accomplishments as an above-average person, as you can in that seemingly safer world of simple routine and simplicity. That life is not safer or happier at all. You are actually more at the mercy of life than you will be through the development of Power-Faith. After you have mastered the ability to function adequately in any situation, to take opportunities and use them to great advantage, and to feel at ease in any strata of life, almost every avenue is open to you. You can go back to the simple life by *choice*. Without those abilities, you would be living a mediocre or inadequate life because you had no choice. It is better to choose than to be resigned to fate.

Just as you read of outstanding people who are unhappy, you read often of successful people who choose to go back to a simple life. You see, the need to accomplish and prove themselves is not as important for those people as just knowing they can if they want to. There is great peace of mind and comfort in knowing that. Many people of great talent and ability find adequate fulfillment in the *faith* they have in their abilities.

Almost without exception, they are people who have adjusted their view of life to the point that they are over-awed by very few things.

What is life really like if it is not a great mystical cosmic order beyond your comprehension?

Life's accomplishments are a series of very small contributions by many different people. One person does not do everything it takes to put together a monumental advancement of man.

Some accomplishments are made over many centuries by men adding tiny bits to the contributions of those before. Other complex achievements are made by many people working at the same time in separate areas of responsibility. If enough men work long enough on a project, the results can be almost beyond man's wildest dreams.

No one person conquered disease. Millions of people worked for centuries to arrive at the place medical science occupies today. The automobile has required tens of thousands of people and a century of progress, one step at a time, to reach the present level of technology. Buildings are built brick by brick, section by section, job by job. No one man builds or designs a large building by himself.

The space industry works on the same principle. Thinking about the space effort as a total program staggers most people's imaginations. Every part of the program represents a tiny contribution by one of many people. The entire project is too big for one person to comprehend, much less create alone. An endeavor of this magnitude has become reality because men have learned how to add up countless contributions by multitudes of people.

Every project of any size is accomplished on that principle. Even families function best when each contributes a portion of the total family life. In fact, man seems to function at his most efficient when he can visualize life in small components, and then harness small contributions from people in great number.

If life seems overwhelming to you, perhaps you need to begin thinking of life in terms of small components rather than in its larger context. That way of seeing life can become an automatic and helpful viewpoint after awhile.

A city may seem frightening in its totality. But a city is simply a large collection of individual persons, small businesses, individual streets, and so on. A city is a collection of small neighborhoods each with its own stores, parks, and schools. Neighborhoods tend to serve the purpose of a community within a city, like a small town within a larger one. That helps make the city more personal and manageable to the residents. They can be members of the city, when it is convenient, and part of the neighborhood community, when that is more appropriate. They have the advantage of the city and the warmth of personal identity with their community. People who have that view and feeling about city life are the ones who appreciate and enjoy the city most. Those who are unhappy in city life are almost always those who see the city as overwhelming in size and complexity.

Many people prefer small-town or rural life for the best and most healthy reasons. Those people are not the ones who need to understand this discussion. People who *escape* to small towns or rural life, because they cannot stand the pressures of urban life, do need to reevaluate their life view. They do not have free choice about where they live or how they function.

You will be most happy and secure when you can handle life in any situation or environment. To be a whole person emotionally, you need confidence to function competently under pressure, or against competition. You need also to have a life view which breaks reality down into its component parts. Small components will not overawe you nearly as often as great complex segments will.

It is important that people today develop an ability to cope with the urban environment. There was a day in America when most people lived in towns or rural areas. Today most people live in cities, and the trend is increasing in that direction. By A.D. 2000, there will be an urban sprawl down the entire East Coast, another stretching from Brownsville, Texas, to the Florida Gulf Coast with Houston, Texas, as the population center. The West Coast will be a continuous city from Seattle to San Diego.

If you cannot cope with urban living, you will be seriously hampered in your ability to enjoy life and function adequately.

You will be able to develop great confidence in yourself only when you can also develop confidence in your surroundings. Power-Faith requires that you have as much faith in your ability to cope with life as you have in your ability to cope with yourself.

God has made life for you. Be at ease in it. If life seems complicated and awesome, just remember that you are more complex than life is. You have more than enough talent, ability, strength, potential, and wisdom to solve anything life can devise.

> We cannot tell what may happen to us in the strange medley of life. But we can decide what happens in us— how we can take it, what we do with it—and that is what really counts in the end. How to take the raw stuff of life and make it a thing of worth and beauty—that is the test of living. *Life is an adventure of faith,* if we are to be victors over it, not victims of it. Faith in the God above us, faith in the little infinite soul within us, faith in life and in our fellow souls—without faith, the plus quality, we cannot really live.
>
> —Joseph Fort Newton

5 Life Is an Adventure of Faith

Jesus was chided several times for picking grain and heal-
ing on the Sabbath. Once he replied: "The sabbath was
made for man, not man for the sabbath" (Mark 2:27).
Jesus clearly shows us God's plan for life in his statement.
If the Sabbath was made for man, what about the other
days of the week? Are they not even more at man's disposal?

I believe it is entirely consistent to expand Jesus' words
to the whole of life:

Life was made for man—not man for life!

That is the fourth point of Power-Faith.

There is all the difference in the world in those two
views of life. Life is at your complete disposal. It is, because God created life that way. You were not created to
fill a predetermined niche in the order of things. You have
not been purposely limited to an average or below-average
life because God needs so many ditch diggers, so many

poor people, so many untalented people, or a certain number of inadequate people.

God has not ordained or set your place in life. You determine your own place in life. There are inadequate people and underachievers in the world because they do not know how to make a better life for themselves. Life was made for you. You may need to get used to watching for opportunities and learning to interpret things as opportunities. Power-Faith has a lot to do with your view of opportunities. As you develop Power-Faith, you will find it helps you interpret opportunities by giving you faith that you can use more situations and ideas to personal advantage. Power-Faith will also help you put opportunity to work by helping discover and develop talents, self-assurance, creativity, and competence.

Building self-assurance, becoming convinced there is a vast reserve of talent, capability, and strength in you—coupled with faith that life was made for you—are giant strides toward realizing the tremendous joy of mastering life.

Jesus speaks to the question of God's providing for man in his Sermon on the Mount (Matthew 6:25–34). Rest assured, He says, that God has designed the world to take care of your needs. If God has created an order of things which will provide for the birds of the air and lilies of the field, how much more is life designed to take care of you.

The principle of life, the way it functions, is a creative one. To live is to make use of things. We breathe air, drink water, and eat what the earth provides. Man uses his brain to fashion from his physical resources, to put his own talents to use, and create useful situations. Living is a process of constantly using opportunities. The most creative people, then, are those who are getting the most out of life. They are taking advantage of the basic life principle: Life was made for man to use. God created everything in life to be used by man for something. To live is to create—one must create to live.

Life is not a matter of sitting back and having all our wants and desires met with a wish or snap of the fingers. Yet every resource for our needs and comfort is provided in the world. Most of the earth's resources, like our own, must be taken in their natural state and fashioned into things which are useful. The entire design of life is to provide unlimited opportunity for men to create from God's basic materials.

"May you live all the days of your life" is an old greeting attributed to Jonathan Swift. It is an ideal to strive for. Life is terribly short. If you waste it away using the tiniest portion of your creative talents, you throw away the great experience of living which God gives only once, and then briefly.

George Bernard Shaw once wrote:

"When I die I want to be thoroughly used up. The harder I work, the more I live. Life is no brief candle for me. It is a sort of splendid torch, which I have got hold of for the moment. I want to make it burn as brightly as possible before handing it on to future generations."

This fourth principle of Power-Faith is an essential addition to developing confidence in your own abilities and talent. If you have faith that everything in life is at your disposal, and that God has planned it this way, you are seeing yourself in a new and magnificent position. All of life is at your feet. You have enough talent and capability to be endlessly creative with life's opportunities.

There is power in that combination of you and life. There is more power than you ever thought you possessed. You stand in an unlimited position of power to deal with life. Moreover, God is pleased that you do. In that position of power over life, you are fulfilling more of the potential God created in you. You are fulfilling the plan God designed for man.

Most people waste too much of the potential God gave man. How can that be good? Certainly God is more pleased to see you using some of the vast resources He gave you than to watch you as you waste life in timid, shallow ways using only the most obvious and easy opportunities of life. It is not selfish to develop your ability to master life. Even as you feel the exhilaration of developing your abilities in life, you are at the same time fulfilling God's plan for you. As you achieve more and more of your potential, you move closer to the goal of being a total person.

Seen in that context, the genius of God's plan for your life becomes more apparent: It is always a thrilling and enrichening experience to fulfill God's plan for you.

I am in strong disagreement with those who believe it is a punishing, self-sacrificing business to follow God's way. What utter nonsense. The great joy of God's plan is that you always receive great fulfillment when you obey His will. To be unselfish brings deep satisfaction. To serve others, even sacrificially, is rewarding.

God's plan enriches you when you give yourself for others, and now we see that His plan also works when you develop the abilities He has given for fulfilling your own life.

Handling life creatively will require some consideration of a practical course of action.

There is an old saying: "Learn from your mistakes." It is not a very good rule, though. All you will learn from your mistakes is what *not* to do again. A much better rule to follow is: "Learn from your successes." Success will teach you more about how to be successful than all the mistakes you could find to study.

You will do better to notice whenever you do something right. Analyze the situation: "What did I do? Why was it effective? How could I apply that to another situation? What is the principle which made this successful?"

You will find it takes two things for success. First, it requires the development of your ability to recognize opportunity creatively.

Dr. Charles L. Allen, the popular pastor of Houston's First United Methodist Church, has written over twenty best-selling books in which he speaks continually of God's power to enhance man's daily life. People frequently ask Dr. Allen what it takes to achieve success. One of the rules he usually cites has to do with learning to judge values. "Every person has a certain amount of enthusiasm," he says. "Enthusiasm is like money. Once you have spent it, it is gone. If you spend all your enthusiasm on something which interests you, but is not very beneficial, you will not have much left to spend on anything else."

Few things are as important in life as learning to make good value judgments. A person's set of values will be as individual as his or her fingerprints. No one else can establish your values for you. They will grow out of your personality and your interests, and be strongly influenced by your talents.

~~Your self-image will also contribute~~ materially to your
values. If you decide something is unattainable, you may
have little interest in pursuing it. You may place it very
low on your value scale because you have the idea it is
beyond your reach. As you ponder your inner potential,
and begin to accept the reality of your abilities in life,
take a careful look at your values. Some of them will
change automatically as your self-image changes. Others
will, just as unconsciously, linger on, unchanged. You may
need to practice thinking bigger. You may need to get
used to looking beyond some interests and goals which
before were adequate to you. Now you may feel confident
to rearrange your values in life, and consider more important goals and aspirations.

A person without much self-confidence may be content
to get by with few close friends because he is afraid to
meet new people. Someone else may find a hobby takes
more of his enthusiasm than his career because he feels
inadequate to advance very far in that occupation or pro-
fession. As self-image and one's view of life change, it may
seem more realistic to believe career opportunities are
possible.

Inner peace and the ability to handle pressure may open
new avenues of interest as life seems more attractive and
less frightening! Do not be hesitant to grow in your interests, as your perspective of life changes. A new you will
require new interests and higher goals to be satisfied.
When your life is thoroughly grounded in Power-Faith,
you will know that higher goals are yours for the taking.
Once it no longer frightens you to think of trying for those
great dreams, you will find deep personal reward in push-
ing out into new interests and achievements.

The interaction between self-image and your view of life is always a factor in your ability to find success. A recent article in the magazine *Psychology Today* reports a significant study by Jeanne Marecek and David Mettee of Yale University. Marecek and Mettee became interested in the fact that psychologists were not able to explain why some people with a poor self-image seem to avoid success at all cost, while others with low self-esteem became quite attracted to success after discovering how rewarding it is.

They had a theory that a couple of factors might explain the paradox. One important factor could be the certainty with which one believes his negative self-image. The other might be whether the person feels responsible for the success he achieves.

The researchers took a group of volunteers who were asked to perform a task. They divided the participants into groups with high self-esteem and low self-esteem. Then they further subdivided the groups according to the degree of certainty about their self-image.

During the task, the researchers did two things. They told half of each group that success depended on blind luck. They told the other half success depended on skill. After the participants began work, they were interrupted about halfway through and everyone was told privately he was doing very well, and was praised.

The results supported Marecek and Mattee's theory. The group with high self-esteem did well. Those with poor self-esteem who thought success depended on blind luck did well, just as those with high self-esteem did. Every group did well except those who were *convinced* of a negative self-image, in the group which was told it took skill to do well. After they were praised, they did worse than before.

We discussed before the psychological barriers concerning self-image. Those were not just exercises in useless information about the mind. This experiment by Marecek and Mettee, and many more which are being made all across the country, are confirming the importance of self-image in determining who you are as a person.

The lesson to remember from the experiment above is that people who are firmly convinced of a negative self-image may avoid success unconsciously because it is not consistent with their view of themselves. If one has a very poor self-image, success may actually be a frightening prospect. They are already familiar with failure and can accept it by reminding themselves: "I knew I would fail; I'm just not an adequate person."

It is less a strain, emotionally, for them to fail and remain consistent with their self-image (it is more comfortable, you could say), and too great a strain emotionally to cope with something as unfamiliar as success. Success for that person is very uncomfortable and frightening. Failure is comfortable and familiar.

Most people have some areas of life in which they feel insecure. You will do well to remember that this marvelous mind God has given man must be understood before it can yield its greatest benefits to you. In this instance, it is important that you know how the mind handles insecurity.

As you consider God's plan for you, and His plan for life to be at your disposal, you may need to focus your new view about you and life upon the level of success you believe you can attain. If you are indeed in possession of tremendous depths of untapped ability and talent, and if

God has made life for you to use, it is not just blind luck that success comes your way when you apply your abilities creatively to life. Many people go through life believing that their success is the result of luck. That is rarely true. Learn to accept your successes as evidence that you are a growing person. You can expand your horizons. You will be a capable person when you begin unlocking the limitless power of God's plan for you.

Even as you enjoy the rewards that come from using your potential more creatively in life, you are without question fulfilling God's plan and dream for you.

6 Any Problem Can Be Solved

I know a lady who is so frightened of freeway driving that she never leaves her little neighborhood within the city. There are stores around the city stocked with merchandise from all over the world, with lower prices than in her neighborhood. There are parks and theaters and delightful restaurants. There are countless opportunities all across the city. She never takes advantage of any of those assets. Her fears and anxieties, and feelings of insecurity, rob her of real free decision. They also rob her of all the wonderful advantages of the city.

Self-confidence and a manageable life-view contribute to solving the problems of urban living. For instance, the person who can look at a neighborhood drug problem and break it down into component, manageable segments, can work effectively toward solutions.

The drug problem has become an emotional issue. To some people, drugs pose a larger-than-life terror. Drugs are very dangerous, but are a conquerable enemy. They

67

possess no superhuman characteristics. Overreacting will be as harmful as underreacting. The key to controlling illegal drug use will be cool-headed analysis, and a great deal of plain, unglamorous, hard work.

The person who sees drug usage as a nebulous, vast national terror is looking at a problem too big to handle. Any problem, such as the current concern over drugs, can be solved only by many people working in very small areas, making many very small contributions. You can manage a neighborhood problem. You cannot take on the world. Nobody requires you to tackle the world. You can solve any problem you have, if you remove it first from any over-awing monster context.

Franklin Roosevelt was incisive when he told America: "The only thing we have to fear is fear itself." The Depression was a psychological phenomenon. It was the same vicious cycle discussed previously in relation to self-image. The Depression involved the national self-image. Failure and inadequacy in the national economy produced poor self-image ("things are bad, the economy is shot, we are in a desperate situation, we can't seem to pull ourselves out, we are going to be ruined"). That produced more failure and inadequacy ("I'd better lay off people, better cut production, better save my money instead of investing, better not buy new equipment"). That worsened the economy and drove the nation into deeper depression.

How did America get back on her feet? In this case, World War II burst upon us, and America discovered an amazing fact. Not only did the nation have the capability for pulling out of depression, but, when suddenly called on to make up for years of neglect and isolationist inattention to world affairs, America responded with an outpouring of productivity that astounded the entire world.

The nation possessed such a great depth of capability and talent that America was able to literally overwhelm the enemy under an avalanche of industry, equipment, new inventions, and dynamic leadership. We were even surprised at ourselves. We couldn't believe our nation, so lately crippled and paralyzed under depression, could do all that.

The relationship between self-image and a realistic view of life is important to understand. It is necessary to work on self-image and on deflating the larger-than-life image of things at the same time. The vicious cycle of inadequate behavior and poor self-image reacting off each other also works in reverse. Adequate behavior contributes to better self-image, and better self-image causes more adequate behavior. Generally, adequate behavior is the breakthrough that makes the first improvement in self-image. Then, better self-image makes it easier to achieve the next level of competent behavior, and soon the cycle is whirling away quite productively.

It may be that you have given larger-than-life properties to the areas of life that most overwhelm you. Have you decided that pressure is something you just cannot cope with? Have you decided that pursuing great dreams would require too much? Are you resigned to the fact that you are not talented enough to compete with others in creative things?

You may need to strip away the mystical, magical, larger-than-life context you have built around your problems, before you can deal with them. There are no superhuman dimensions to any problem in personality development.

Look at the way people react to unexpected situations. Some situations scare people more than others. We have programmed ourselves to be almost hysterically afraid of some emergencies.

Snakebite paralyzes most people with sheer terror. A minor traffic accident causes many people to become hysterical or to experience severe psychological shock. Cancer terrifies people.

Analyzed calmly, terror or hysterics will worsen any of those possibilities. Most snakebites simply require medication and careful bed rest until the system has disposed of the snake's venom. In America, snakebites are rarely fatal.

Traffic accidents can unnerve a person far beyond the actual cuts and bruises. People involved in fairly minor traffic accidents will take days or weeks to get back to normal.

Doctors say that hysteria resulting from discovery of cancer can be one of the most destructive handicaps to restoring good health. A great proportion of cancer is cured today, but the word strikes terror in the minds of many people.

Snakebites, traffic accidents, cancer, and many more things in life would do much less damage if they were accepted with less panic, hysteria, and terror. It is the terror which makes many minor or manageable emergencies become major problems.

Mind-set has a great deal to do with how serious a problem really is. A bump on the head, sore muscles, a cut that requires a few stitches, a bruised hip, a broken bone, are major concerns to many people. On the other hand, a professional football player may have any, or all, of those ills and go right on functioning normally with little awareness of them. Of course, you know why: He has programmed his mind to disregard most physical injuries. He has raised his body tolerance and his ability to handle physical injury psychologically. He can actually function close to normal, when the same injury would be a major problem and impair your normal behavior drastically.

In a sense, professional football players ignore injury and pain. Injuries which would dominate your thinking or seriously impair your behavior may be almost ignored by the athlete because they do not scare him. A broken bone is just a broken bone, not a national emergency. Bruises and sore muscles, which leave us racked with pain, are ignored by someone who treats them as little nuisances and nothing more.

Contrast that with the behavior of many people down with a cold or the flu. They require being waited on hand and foot. They want to be fussed over, made much of, babied, and constantly cared for. Could it be that sickness is a way people have for gaining a little attention in a world of pressures and demands? Could people find better ways than sickness to get attention and concern?

Mental attitudes *definitely* control physical behavior and even physical bodily functions. Any doctor will tell you that a person's mental attitude largely determines his ability to fight disease, injury, or emotional problems. Doctors estimate that 60 percent to 80 percent of the problems they see are psychosomatic. The illnesses are real all right. The people are *not* just pretending to be sick. But, actual physical illness can be caused psychologically.

A man who deals in large business ventures may make and lose several fortunes, or face successions of good and bad times because he is not panicked by large sums of money or by financial reverses. How many people have tried once to invest in the stock market, lost money, and said: "Never again!" then spent the rest of their lives afraid to consider any sort of investment. No one with wealth could have afforded that attitude.

Any problem is worse:

1. When you allow it to take on larger-than-life proportions.
2. When it scares you so badly you react in sheer terror or in a hysterical manner.
3. When you allow the problem to become a vast nebulous monster over which you have no control.

When you react to life hysterically, you run the risk of acting on emotion rather than good judgment. Your personal problems, just as surely as the nation's, will be much more manageable when they are seen in a realistic, commonsense context.

When anything overawes you, it is a sign you are succumbing to the tendency to attach mystical properties to that situation or person. Famous people are no different than you, except that they have worked hard to develop their talents or struck it lucky. (Usually both are necessary to become famous.) Professions and social strata are simply things to be mastered. With enough faith in yourself, and enough faith that everything in life is at your disposal, you can master the most thrilling goals imaginable.

If life is too big and complicated, break it down into manageable components and begin mastering small things until you have built up a backlog of accomplishment.

Alcoholics Anonymous is the only organization that effectively works with serious drinking problems. It teaches the alcoholic to break down his problem into small manageable segments. "One day at a time," is a slogan of A.A. "Don't worry about staying sober the rest of your life," they tell their members, "just worry about today. Stay sober today. Tomorrow, worry about that one day. Just one day at a time."

Lifetime sobriety is more than most alcoholics can visualize, much less handle. A person can understand and handle sobriety for one day, though. In a very real way, Alcoholics Anonymous is teaching its members to make their problem manageable. They help strip away the overwhelming size and staggering scope, and they help remove the myth that the problem is bigger than the person. Once a problem is manageable, then you can begin to manage it.

A church paper I received recently contained this little story about bicycle riding:

> Those who ride bicycles say that it is easier to ride up a hill at night than it is during daylight. Hills that are practically impossible of ascent may be negotiated at night. At night the cyclist can see but a few feet in front of him, and the faint light of his lantern gives him the illusion that the hill is either level or not steep. He feels that he can go the few feet more than his light shows, and in this manner keeps on and on, while in the daytime he sees the whole hill, the whole problem, and it seems so steep to climb that his courage fails him.

The psychology of problem solving is a concept you should understand fully:

1. Strip away any mystical properties you may have attached to your problem. Don't let problems become fuzzy, hard-to-define terrors that lurk in the back of your mind. Don't attach superhuman powers to your problem.
2. Break down your problem into its smallest components. Then begin solving one small segment at a time.

The most common reason for problems going unsolved is that people are not willing to put out the long-term hard work and determination to get the job done.

You can do anything you set your mind to, if you are willing to pay the price!

Life is at your disposal. There is nothing overawing about any phase of life unless you let it be. High goals can be achieved. Large problems can be solved. Obstacles can be overcome if you will have faith that God has intended for all of life to be available for your use.

7 Let Life Say Yes to You

There are six principles of Power-Faith. We have discussed four so far. It might be helpful to summarize them here:

1. Your self-image determines who you really are. Who you are will always be consistent with who you *think* you are.
2. You are using only a tiny fraction of the potential within you. You are an underachiever, not a limited person.
3. You must overcome your awe of life before you can master it.
4. Life was made for man, not man for life. You are actually fulfilling God's plan for you as you learn to cope with life successfully.

Think back over these first four principles and it becomes apparent that one cannot talk about any area of

Power-Faith separately. All of the points above apply
equally to the discussions of you, life, and God's power.
Self-image, for instance, keeps reappearing through the
chapters. You cannot understand your own mind unless
you understand the role your self-image plays; nor can
you comprehend God's plan for life unless you see the importance of self-image in dealing with life's situations. You
will not be able to accept the reality of God's power in
your life unless your self-image includes an understanding
that you are a child of God, and share the same life-force
which *is* God.

The strength of Power-Faith is to redirect your thinking,
so that you come to know yourself as a totally unlimited
person. You are unlimited in your personal abilities to be
creative, to handle pressures, to develop confidence, and
so on. You are unlimited in life because God designed life
to be the resource material for your creativity. By God's
own promise, you have an unlimited relationship with
Him. He is continually with you, a part of you, giving
you open access to an existence beyond mortal limits.

You have every right to become excited as you consider
the possibilities for Power-Faith to open new vistas of living. Confidence in a new you expands your need for room
to grow. Your imagination can only begin to see the possibilities which grow out of the assurance that life is designed to provide unlimited opportunity and endless raw
materials.

You have discovered by now that Power-Faith is not a
psychology book. All of these factors of the mind, and of
the materials of life, must be seen in a perspective of
Christian faith before they can yield man their ultimate
meaning. The design of the human mind is God's. It is

as much a study of God's power to learn how the mind manages the body as it is to study God in the Bible. To talk about life as limitless opportunity is to speak of God's will. Everything within the Christian tradition convinces me that life is intended to be utilized by man through endless creativity.

To maintain that God's power can add an infinite depth to the power man possesses is simply to affirm the words of Christ and the weight of Christian doctrine.

Power-Faith is a Christian context for living. It is an entirely optimistic view of life. It is a faith grounded in the honest belief that you are a person of undreamed potential. It is faith in the basic goodness of life through God's design. Power-Faith calls you to see the possibility for living which God has planned for you, set against the pitifully small attempt most people make.

Lack of confidence and a mystical awe of life confine and cripple most people into a very limited existence. The gist of Power-Faith is this: No one is limited to an inadequate life. The bounds of your limits are so far above anything you have ever achieved you cannot yet see them.

The very sad fact is that most people never understand the scope of their abilities.

Henry L. Mencken, the noted author, once received a note from a woman serving time in a state prison. She was on death row waiting to be executed. She wrote to say she had read his book, *In Defense of Woman*. Then she added this tragic sentence: "If I had only known how smart I was, I would not be here now."

Life is designed to say yes. Oh, there are certainly times when life is difficult and tragic. That is because life is impartial by design. The laws God has devised will function whether we men approve or not. The dependability of God's laws is necessary. Most of the time, it is comforting and essential that the laws which govern the world always work predictably. There are those times when life deals you a cruel blow, however, and God has taken that into account. It is an integral part of Power-Faith to know that God provides for every situation, no matter how difficult or tragic, to bring forth good in some manner.

The death of a loved one can teach faith, or humility, or perhaps appreciation for loved ones still around. It might develop strength, self-reliance, or patience.

A business reverse might bring a man and wife closer together than ever before. It might open new horizons for opportunity. The good does not do away with the bad. It can temper the bad, though, and on occasion eventually outweigh the bad. God places that possibility in every situation.

Much has been written about saying yes to life. You must understand with real faith that life is first saying yes to you. What can you say yes to, if you do not believe life responds to your open arms?

Get rid of your awe of life. Know that life is the raw material of opportunity. Understand that life is saying yes to you and was before you were even aware of what life is about. The design of life is a direct and thorough openness.

Are you that far along in your faith? Then, and not until then, are you ready to say your yes to life.

Hard work has already been mentioned as necessary to getting most things in life. Sure determination is also vital. How badly do you want something? How sure are you that it is something you must have?

An old story of the Depression days has stayed in my mind for years. It tells of a young couple who knocked on the door of a preacher's house one evening and asked to be married. The minister called his wife to witness the ceremony. The young man and woman were radiant as the preacher began, "Dearly beloved, we are gathered here . . ."

They exchanged their vows with great joy showing from within, so that the preacher and his wife, who shared many such events, were quite impressed with the couple's obvious love for each other.

As the newlyweds left, the young man handed the minister a rather disheveled envelope. On it was written in pencil: "For The Minister." Inside the house, the minister opened the flap and took out a crumpled old dollar bill and a scrawled pencil note which read: "Dear Sir, I wish I could give you more for marrying us, but I only had two dollars. This leaves us one dollar to get started on."

You know what? I bet they made it.

One of the most common reasons for failure is that people give up too easily. Whatever your goals—confidence to meet new people, to handle pressure, to hold your temper, become successful in a career or avocation—they all require hard work. A clue to success is that most people *will* be lazy in pursuing their goals. Extra work on your part, then, will be doubly fruitful. While you are perfecting your skills and moving toward your own goal fulfillment, you will at the same time be moving beyond those around you, in part because they are allowing you by their laxness.

Several years ago, I found a quaint old book in a second-hand bookshop. It is bound in leather and was published

in 1876. It is called *The Royal Path of Life,* by T. L. Haines
and L. W. Yaggy. The language is stilted and old-fash-
ioned. So are many of the ideas in it. Still, there is a certain charm in the old book. The chapter titled "Opportunity" contains these thoughts which are still good
advice:

> Great opportunities are generally the result of the wise
> improvement of small ones. Wise men make more oppor-
> tunities than they find. If you think your opportunities
> are not good enough, you had better improve them . . . .
> As a general rule, those who have no opportunities despise
> small ones; and those who despise small opportunities
> never get large ones.

Do you think your opportunities are limited? You cannot conquer the world because you must deal in small,
mundane matters all day? That old homily from a forgot-
ten book calls you back to a more truthful attitude about
your situation. If you do well with small opportunities,
they will help large opportunities to come your way. If
you decide that a task or responsibility is menial and
would be a waste of much endeavor, you fall into one of
the most common traps in life.

That convenient rationalization has deprived people of
more opportunity than any other single influence.

Even if a great opportunity does come your way despite
your attitude concerning lesser things, you may be so un-
practiced at doing a job well that the great chance is
muffed. Self-discipline, determination, self-denial, and
easy administration are not mastered on the spur of a
moment. Many great opportunities have been lost because

the person was not prepared to capitalize on the opportunity properly.

That may sound very dull and "square." It is an attitude which is essential to making opportunity work for you, however. Those character traits are actually keys to freedom and success. They only seem to tie one down. They only appear to be dull. They are the personal requirements for achieving success. You must believe they are essential, and live them, to become successful at anything in life.

Shirley Price might have decided early in life that her opportunities and abilities were too limited to have any dreams at all. She could have been easily excused for that attitude, and no one would have blamed her at all. You see, Shirley was born without any arms.

Happily, living on charity and pity was not at all enough for Shirley. She learned to write and work mathematics with her feet. She became an honor graduate of her high school, graduated from Texas Southern University, and became an employee of the Manned Spacecraft Center. There she does secretarial and clerical work, as well as computer work.

Shirley was recently selected as the Outstanding Handicapped Federal Employee of the Year. Her award was presented by the President's wife at the White House.

Learning to swim is high on the list of priorities Shirley has planned for the future. She already sews, irons, and cooks. She is an accomplished singer and has gained widespread recognition for her musical talents independent of her other accomplishments.

The crowning touch came when the city commissioners of Hitchcock, Texas, her hometown, proclaimed the third week of April "Shirley Price Week."

Did Shirley accomplish what she has because her opportunities were greater than the average person? Of course not. Did she do it on luck, and whim, and no hard work? Again, she obviously could not have. Those "square" attributes of hard work and determination are not prisons to deprive you of the freedom to live. They are your keys to success. You can accomplish any dream you can imagine if you have enough determination, and avoid that most common trap of laziness toward whatever opportunities are presented to you.

There are enough reserves of untapped potential within you that even without arms, you can reach great heights. What can you do with the opportunities you have?

8 The Fun Is in the Running

The New Testament seems very clear in its teachings that life is basically good. Christ, John, and Paul all speak of God's will as being a rewarding discipline for life. The one aspect of life common to all the New Testament writers and clearly voiced by Jesus is that the joy of life is in the living of it. If that sounds a bit too obvious, consider it this way: Accomplishment is certainly satisfying, but sometimes when our goals are achieved, we look back wistfully to the fun we had in getting there.

Walt Kelly, creator of the comic strip "Pogo," is widely regarded for the incisive views of life contained in his wit and humor. In an essay on the function of humor he once wrote:

> Too soon we breast the tape and too late we realize the fun lay in the running . . . . If there is any satisfaction in life it must come in transit, for who can tell when he will be struck down in mid-method?

The greatest mistake made by many people is their failure to enjoy today just for itself. Today is too often just preparation for tomorrow. "Tomorrow will be a better day. Tomorrow we will really start to live," is their outlook. Sometimes year after year goes by without really being enjoyed. People frequently ask: "Where have the years gone? Time just seems to fly by." One reason is that they didn't really "live" enough of those years. It was always "tomorrow" they were going to start enjoying life.

"After I get out of school, I will really have it made. When I get that raise, we can relax and enjoy life a little. When the kids are through college, we can finally do a little living. When we retire, we are going to enjoy doing all those things we never had time to do before."

Sound familiar? How much of your life is being wasted preparing for some utopian tomorrow? Waiting for adulthood, waiting for graduation, waiting for a job, a raise, a promotion, a new house, getting the kids raised—suddenly the years have flown by and you haven't really lived any of them as fulfilling experiences in themselves. They were all endured, or tolerated as preparation for the future.

And then one day, tomorrow doesn't come for you in this life. It is all over, and your life was never really lived. It was a long process of waiting so you could live tomorrow.

It is not the *accomplishment* which gives most frequent meaning to your years, but the *accomplishing*. The goal achieved is the special frosting on your cake, but life for most people is spent more in trying than in moments of victory. As important as it is to accomplish your goals in life, it is no less important that every day be lived and savored, in and for itself.

Okay, you don't make enough money to cruise around the world, or own a ski lodge in the mountains. Enjoy what you have now. Live as you can live. Don't sulk because you cannot live as you wish you could. Today is its own gift. It is not a throwaway in preparation for some future day.

You may need to adjust your mental attitude about life. A great many people have become almost wholly oriented toward the future. It is quite a common view of life. Spend a little time rearranging your thinking to enjoy today, and this year, in your present situation. Life will perk up considerably, even dramatically.

Actually, life gets very boring when it is all a preparation for the future. It can become boring little by little without your becoming aware of it. By reassigning a new value on the living of a day or a year, you can make the experience of living it justification enough. You are not required to justify today by making it a preparation for tomorrow. The preparation involved in living today is above and beyond the basic experience of having one day of life.

Ideally, then, today is both an end in itself and a means to an end. People get into trouble when they try to make life one or the other exclusively. Some people are inclined to see life as one long fling at enjoyment and self-satisfaction. Others let life slip through their fingers because they are always preparing for tomorrow.

God has designed life to be most rewarding when a balance is drawn between the two functions of life.

A woman came to me and confided that her whole adult

life had been spent living for her children. Her first duty had been always to them, she said. As the years went by, she told herself there would be plenty of time to think of herself and do the things she dreamed of after they had gone. She spent her youth, then her middle years, with one interest in life—her children.

Finally they were all grown, and gone from her home to raise families of their own. Now that she had accomplished her task, she found herself in a very different situation than she had imagined. She had spent so long living for her children that she had never learned how to live for herself. Now without the children to give her life meaning, she was lost and perplexed. She found she did not have any real interests in life. She was despondent and lonely because she felt as though life was over for her.

We had to go back to explore some of the values she had formed about life. A discussion of the two functions of living helped her see the mistake she had made. The woman thought it out for herself after we had talked awhile. It was she who suggested that, in spite of the best intentions, she had spent a great part of her life waiting to live at some later date. When that day finally came, she suddenly realized she did not know how to go about living for herself.

"Well," she said finally, "I've wasted too much time already. I need to get out there and start learning how to live for myself, and enjoy it."

An older minister offered some excellent advice once, about finding fulfillment in the pastorate.

"When I first entered the ministry," he said, "I looked on every church I pastored as just a stepping-stone to the next one. The next one would be a little bit bigger, a little further up the ladder, and would pay a little more salary. That was a mistake.

"I wasn't really happy at any of those churches because I was always pointing toward the next one. I was sure I would be happy if I could just get to that next larger church. When I got there, though, I found that wasn't enough either. There was always another promotion out there somewhere.

"Finally, I happened into a church that was so much fun, so rewarding and enjoyable that I began to experience a satisfied contentment I had never had before. Without realizing it at first, I learned a valuable lesson. With a different attitude, I could have enjoyed every church that much. Instead, I had just endured them until something better came along.

"I learned how important mental attitude is to enjoying life. Since I stopped looking on every pastorate as a stepping-stone to the next, I have loved every place I have been, and actually found it was not as important to get on to the next one as it used to be."

That advice and experience is shared by men in every occupation. A job will be much more rewarding if a person "lives" in it and enjoys life right there, today. Resenting one's present position in life, and pointing always to a brighter tomorrow, will rob life of much of its luster.

Adequate preparation for tomorrow can be made without sacrificing the enjoyment of living today just for itself. Isn't that what Jesus really meant when he said: "Therefore I tell you, do not be anxious about your life, what you shall eat or what you shall drink, nor about your body, what you shall put on. Is not life more than food, and the body more than clothing" (Matthew 6:25)?

9 Dare To Live

It is exciting to think of yourself as a person with great potential and power. Then, when you begin to see life as opportunity endlessly available to you, and yourself as someone equipped to take advantage of life, the picture begins to be even more exciting. When, on top of that, you know that this dynamic concept of you is God's optimistic hope for your life, the idea is almost staggering.

If you have never considered yourself in these terms before, it will take some time for all that to sink in. Once you have absorbed this new understanding of yourself, in relation to life and God, it is time to move on to consideration of how you will begin living as this new you.

We are now leaving the discussions of how to see yourself in a new light, and how to see life as being available for you. It is time to begin preparing to live in this new context. For all the joy there is in discovering the infinite resources within yourself, living the *new you* is even more thrilling. Doing it is more fun than discovering it.

The fifth principle of Power-Faith speaks to an essential fact of life which you need to keep in mind as you look to the future. It sounds too simple, but it is actually a profound truth about living.

The fifth principle is: *Security can only come from within.*

Since most people are short on inner security, they tend to spend much of their lives searching for it. The constant quest for security is one of the most basic pursuits of man. People can get quite frantic in their desperation to be secure in life.

Lack of security can be so frightening that it can override all of the wonderful things in life. A person can be quite richly blessed but believe life to be terrible, if he is insecure.

Inner security, or inner peace, can *only* come from within yourself. The mistake most people make is their belief that security can be found in things around them. If inner security eludes a person, it is an easy temptation to look outside for substitutes.

It is one of man's most common faults that he attempts to shortcut the development of personal strength and inner peace with an easy way out. That easy way is to gather things about oneself which will substitute for one's lack of security within.

I know a young man whose security lies in his little hometown. He is not a man of great self-confidence. He needs the comfort of living near his parents, in the familiar environment of his boyhood life. What would happen if his company transferred him to New York City, or Seattle, Washington? My guess is that he would find his security destroyed. He would be frightened and very insecure.

Now suppose he developed great confidence in himself as a person of worth and ability. Suppose he developed a real Power-Faith attitude toward himself and life. New York City could be his "oyster" just as easily as that little hometown. New cities, new opportunities, new experiences might become rewarding delights instead of frightening enemies.

There is an important reason that security from outside is inferior to inner security. If you surround yourself with security, it can be taken away from you! If you develop confidence in yourself as someone who can cope with life in any situation, then it matters much less what setting you are in, for you are the same person no matter what the outward circumstances. It is a serious mistake to think you can substitute for inner security.

Some people create security in their patterns of living. Others find security in a particular job, or familiar surroundings. There are two types of false security which are even more dangerous.

One is the attitude that very few new ideas are going to be allowed into a person's thinking. Many narrow-minded people are really protecting their lack of inner security by seeking security in an unchanging view of life. New ideas and principles frighten them because they upset that comfortable, secure outlook on life which has become their substitute for inner confidence and peace. They not only want to remain unchanged, but actually *need* to be nongrowing to protect their security. That is why narrow-minded people are frequently so difficult to deal with when new ideas are being discussed.

Another dangerous substitute is the practice of protecting oneself from failure, or from the pressures of success,

by refusing to set goals very high. It is a threat to security
if an insecure person fails at something. That outlook on
life dictates to a person that security can best be maintained by sticking to very limited goals and ambitions.
Then one never risks failure. Remember, we have already
seen that some people find success as frightening as failure. It is a scary prospect to some people to face the emotional pressures of success.

The important rule to remember is that success and
failure are only frightening to someone who lacks self-
confidence.

Risk is one of the necessary elements in life. Risk is a
part of living. Risk is one of the factors of life which must
be dealt with as you overcome your awe of life. You have
to lessen your fear of risk as a part of accepting life in
Power-Faith terms. If you have developed confidence in
yourself as an adequate person, and confidence in God's
design for life, success and failure become possibilities
which do not frighten you.

A couple I know owned a store in which they both
worked six days a week. The store brought a meager in-
come. For years, they reconciled themselves to their rather
unrewarding life because they were unwilling to risk what
security they had for a better life. Finally, they decided
to do something about it. They decided between themselves that they had the business skills, the confidence, and
determination to climb out of their rut. After careful research of marketing and sales potential, they sold their
store and bought a general store in the mountains of
Colorado. Their careful planning and years of business
experience proved adequate. Now they are enjoying life
as they had never dreamed a few years ago.

The most rewarding element of their new life is the self-confidence they have found in themselves. Their security lies within now. They would be less likely to buckle under failure now than they would have been if the former business had failed. They are stronger people because they have found that risking has made them stronger inside.

Once again it becomes apparent that God has designed life so that everything is useful to man. There is uncertainty in risks, but God has also assured that risking becomes a valuable tool. Risk develops inner strength. A person who risks cannot expect his security to lie in safe, familiar patterns of living, or in familiar surroundings. Risking teaches self-reliance. It develops toughness for coping with problems and failures. The no-risk life leaves a person weak and vulnerable to fear and insecurity.

A man who loved teaching found himself leaving the classroom and accepting a minor administrative position because it meant financial security for his family. He was unhappy and bored with his job. He longed for something more rewarding and challenging. After long discussion with his family, he began looking for new opportunities. Recently he accepted a position as teacher and assistant administrator of an English-speaking school in Europe. Making the move involved some risk. The family talked over all the pros and cons. Finally they decided the rewards were worth the risk. He wrote me after they had been overseas about eighteen months:

"I have never enjoyed my work as much as I do now, and our family has certainly never been happier . . . . Every week brings a new experience . . . . It's great fun being back in the classroom again . . . . I often remem-

ber the life we were living and thank God we decided to
do something."

You don't have to move to Europe or the Colorado
Rockies to begin *living*. Many exciting opportunities like
those are available across the world, but opportunities are
also available right where you are now.

A hometown or familiar setting is not automatically bad.
It is only a problem if it becomes a security substitute
which robs you of opportunities from the world at large.

The constant need to protect and reinforce security can
become a substitute for living. You begin ruling out one
opportunity after another because they seem always to
have some catch or provision which would threaten your
secure little world. People get into a habit of turning down
opportunities to protect their security, and eventually do
it instinctively, without even thinking about it. I have
tried to help people with that outlook on life and found
it very frustrating.

A person may think he wants help in making life more
meaningful, but then turn down every suggestion for one
reason or another. Remember those pike in the story earlier? A habit of making excuses to protect security can
develop a blind spot to opportunity after awhile. Turning
down opportunities can become automatic. It becomes an
instinctive reflex to think of a good excuse to say no. Finally an even better defense becomes apparent. You grow
conveniently blind to opportunity.

Inner security offers a vast freedom to live! It frees you
to seek out the fulfilling and meaningful things. It frees
you to live moment by moment, to gain from life as well
as giving to it.

Life is slipping too quickly past many people because

they do not live life as it was intended—moment by moment. The spontaneity of life is its most intriguing aspect. In the midst of details of daily living and the worries of job, family, and community, many people have missed the boat on how to enjoy life.

I am not suggesting for a minute that life should be a whimsical romp through trivia and fantasy. Even the serious things in life can be rewarding, though.

Living life moment by moment does take courage. The security of sameness and predictability are alluring sirens that call enticingly to the insecure, through the noise and confusion of today's complex society. Sameness and predictability are comforting in the midst of change and disorder. They become treacherous friends if you rely too heavily on them, however. Your mind can become drugged with the opium of security and soon your predictable friends begin to rob you of the spontaneity of life.

Before long, you can find yourself in a very difficult position. You become more and more involved with protecting your safe life. Like a drug habit, security from the outside requires larger and larger amounts of your mental energy.

Patterns of life and surroundings can change. If your emotional peace of mind rests outside yourself, you are always at the mercy of a changing world. As life grows more complex and change comes more frequently, you must struggle harder to protect your comfortable world. You are not really living; you are too busy protecting the status quo of your security.

People mistakenly assume that high moments are the *exceptions* in life. The assumption is that exciting things only occur once or twice, usually when they are young and still unencumbered with the staidness that seems to creep in with the years.

You may envy people with the courage to plunge exuberantly into life. That courage you envy comes from their inner security. They are not worried about changing surroundings, new patterns of living, or other adjustments. They carry their security inside themselves. They have faith in themselves, in life, and in God's presence in the world.

Many people are living life to the fullest. They have dared; they have risked; they have searched and acted. They are reaping the rich rewards life offers because they possess the faith that unlocks the potential of life. They fairly glow in the spontaneity of fulfilling occupations and creative living.

One family came to life when they took over most of the household chores to let Mom go back to school. Last June, Mom graduated as a Doctor of Medicine. At graduation, the family members were all there to watch. It had been a long, hard struggle. They had all gotten tired and cross at times because of the extra burdens imposed by Mom's heavy school load and long hours. Every time they called a family council to discuss the situation, they all arrived at the same conclusion over again: They were proud of Mom. They wanted to share in helping her do this which was so important to her. It had become important to all of them. Now it was a family goal and everyone wanted to see the goal achieved.

It was a great day when Mom walked across that stage. She took the diploma, but every member of the family felt a personal thrill. It was a triumph for each one, as well as for Mom. Remember, the fun in life is frequently in the running!

Bringing a dream to life, even through sacrifice and hardship, can be as joyous a part of living as the sharing of its fulfillment.

People enjoy reading of others who tour Europe on fifty dollars and a bicycle, purchase their own island, or renovate an eighteenth century barn from which a charming New England home emerges. There are so many ways to enjoy life. The experiences of people who have learned how to let go and live usually glow with enthusiasm and exuberance.

The trouble with too many people is that they feel a momentary thrill, and temptation toward that fulfilling way of living, then sigh wistfully and trudge right back into their hectic and unrewarding life because it is safe and familiar.

A young businessman recently left his construction firm to purchase the patent rights for a new plastics product. He is busily organizing a company to promote and sell it.

"I don't dream casually," he commented. "Dreams are money, but a lot of people don't put any action to them. Many dreamers are too lazy to do anything about their dreams."

Incidentally, experts say his product may revolutionize several areas of the construction business.

For every person who has climbed a mountain, gone to Europe on a shoestring, bought an island, learned to ski, run for public office, shared in ghetto work, gone back to school, found that new career, or broken some old confining condition of life, there are scores more who wish and dream and never act.

My dad is a college professor. Occasionally he enjoys working out in industry during the summer, doing research. It gives him and Mother a nice change of pace.

One summer I was faced with the dreary prospect of working to raise money for college in the fall. The family was spending the summer in Portland, Oregon. It looked like three months of sacking groceries or clerking in a store.

While we were driving through Yellowstone National Park, we discovered that most of the jobs in the hotels and stores are taken by college students in the summer. I decided on the spur of the moment to see if anything was available.

Up at the old Mammouth Hot Springs Hotel, the Yellowstone Park Company had an employment office. I inquired about openings and was told all the jobs had been filled for months. Just as we were leaving, the interviewer remembered that a young man had not shown up over at the Old Faithful Lodge.

"It isn't much of a job," he told me. "You would be a kitchen helper, but you might move up to something better before the summer is over."

A quick family conference settled the matter. Off came my gear, and the family drove out of the park without me. It was a lonesome feeling to watch that car disappear down the road. There I was, two thousand miles from home and stuck for three months.

It was the most thoroughly enjoyable summer I ever spent.

By the summer's end, I was a fry cook on the short order counter. I had earned more than enough for the fall tuition, and learned to cook as well. During those months in Yellowstone, I climbed mountains in the Grand Tetons, rode horseback in the Montana high country, hiked the back trails of Yellowstone Park, swam in the Firehole River, played in snow in July, and made more friends than I had ever imagined, friends from every state in the country.

That experience taught me a valuable lesson about life. It taught me that risking security on the outside can build a better kind of security on the inside. The delightful blessing of God's design is that you will enjoy life the most when you are daring and growing.

10 It's Worth the Risk

A good friend of mine confided to me during his senior year in college that he was thinking of becoming a minister. In the course of our conversation, I asked him where he was planning to take his seminary training.

"Oh, I guess I'll just go to school close to home," he said. "It will be easy to get in and it won't cost very much."

Now this friend was an exceptional person. He had maintained almost straight A's in college and would be graduating near the top of his class. Besides his scholarly abilities, he was a likeable and well-rounded young man.

"Why don't you try for one of the really outstanding universities?" I urged him. "Most guys would give anything to go to a top university, but can't because they don't have the grades to do it. Here you are with all the prerequisites and you are going to settle for less. What can you lose by trying?" I went on. "Write to some of them and see what they say."

For several weeks I pushed and prodded. Here was a

guy with the intellectual ability and the background to do well in even the most demanding university program. It would be a shame for him to breeze through a curriculum that did not really test his ability, when he had so much potential.

He was hesitant and timid about applying to other colleges. The famous names awed him, and I am sure he was thinking, "I could never be accepted into those universities. It's too hard to get in. Why waste my time?"

The process of convincing my friend to make some applications was the same process discussed earlier about overcoming one's awe of life. He had trouble seeing himself worthy of acceptance into the awesome and venerated great universities. "Other people" graduated from those universities.

That is the attitude about life which keeps so many people from setting their sights high enough. "Other people" become doctors, or lawyers, or college graduates, or Ph.D.'s, or successful persons. "Other people" overcome inferiority complexes, or learn to handle any kind of pressure, or be at peace inside. There may be areas of life you dream of conquering which, after awhile, become too overawing and seem above your capability. Living this Power-Faith attitude you develop will require that you believe every level of life is open to you.

One evening, my friend called with some news. He was so excited he could hardly talk to me. "Guess what," he shouted excitedly. "I've been accepted at Yale University. Can you believe it?"

I could believe it. He was certainly qualified for a college of that stature. The task had been to convince my friend of his ability.

Once you have developed faith in your ability to function successfully in life, go out and do it! Begin trying doors. Every door will not open to you, but some doors will. Sometimes you only need one door to open. That one break can set up a whole new life for you.

Don't just dream about it. Begin to live. Begin to attack life boldly and confidently. Make life as full and rich as possible. Tailor life to your needs and talents, but begin to involve yourself with the possibilities that are open to you.

Keep in mind the old saying: "Nothing ventured, nothing gained." It may sound trite after all these years, but it has stuck around because of its basic truth.

One of the most exuberant persons I know is a woman named Margie. She is in her 50s, and as young inside as anyone I have ever known. Margie knows how to live. Her enthusiasm is contagious. People enjoy being around Margie.

It took a good many years for Margie to find the confidence and inner security to begin looking for deeper meaning and new adventure in life. She had always been a religious person, but there seemed to be something missing for her. She discovered a few years ago that she had always let others do her thinking about the Christian gospel. She accepted the answers others passed down to her because she felt she had very little to contribute to religious thought.

One day, says Margie, she woke up to the fact that she was obedient but shallow in her religious practices. She decided she needed to get more involved in finding out just what God meant in her life. She began reading, talking, asking questions, and reevaluating her views. She got involved in her community. She began to go places and see new faces. She found a world of new experiences.

Margie discovered there was a need for adult workers with young people. Before long, she was actively involved in youth work. She became a favorite of the teen-agers because she had an enthusiasm for living which captured their imagination.

Margie is a familiar person across the state now. Her charisma with youth makes her a valuable resource person. She is a woman of boundless energy. Sometimes the young people with whom she works find themselves hard put to keep up Margie's fast pace. She exudes an enthusiasm for living coupled with a great compassion for people.

The enjoyment people find when they are with Margie comes from her apparent joy of living. There is no need to settle for less in life. There are so few Margies in the world. There is no particular reason for that, except for most people's willingness to settle for less. Any life which is dull and boring, any that settles for the least in life, is giving away without need the greatest gift of all—the thrill of living life to the fullest.

Let Margie serve as a living example to you that the spontaneous, joyous life is the most fulfilling. The comfortable lure of safeness and predictability rob life of its joy.

When emotions are pampered for reasons of security, the serious danger which results is very grave. If you go out of your way to keep life bland and predictable, you will never develop any reserves of emotional energy. Those reserves are vital when you encounter unforeseen problems and adversity.

Without those reserves of emotional energy, and the ability to face success and failure without fear, you can be shattered emotionally by crises and adversity. Your pampered and shallow emotions will struggle briefly to cope with the situation. They will be quickly drained. Your lack of experience with uncertainty and risk will leave you open to great fears. Suddenly the cardboard house of safe, protective patterns of living crumbles under the pressure of life, and you are overwhelmed.

In that situation, you are not the master of life. Life has become your master. You cannot substitute for inner security. There *is* no substitute. Developing inner confidence and peace of mind free you to live as joyously as Margie and all the others who have learned the lesson of mastering life.

"Boy, that first experience in business almost stopped me for good," a man told me one evening. "I kept hearing about all these guys who had gone into business for themselves and did just great, so I decided I could do as well as any of them. I went in debt up to my ears to buy a food franchise and off I went. Well, it turned out that nobody was very interested in the stuff I had to sell. The parent company had done a great job of selling me a bill of goods. I lost my shirt."

He talked for awhile about the struggle he had getting back on his feet, but then he mentioned something that really caught my attention.

"The problems we had because of that business failure were terrible at the time," he said, "but I think it was probably worth the setback just for what I learned about being afraid. You know, it might sound a little funny, but that mess helped me get over being so afraid of failing.

"That business failure really put us in a bind, but we worked right out of it, and it wasn't nearly as terrifying as I thought at first. For a little while, though, I was ready to throw in the towel. I think now I could handle almost anything that came along. I got over being so afraid of life. I found out you can handle anything as long as you don't panic."

He is now running a very successful business and says he is actually glad for the experience of the ill-fated franchise. He feels that he will be better able to cope with any future problems because they won't frighten him as they would have before.

Now contrast that story with another man who has talked with me over and over about how much he would like to go into business for himself. He is a school teacher. This man has been talking about his dream of a business for himself for ten years. He hasn't got the courage to get past the talking stage, though. He has the ability to tackle a project on his own, but he is timid about risking. How often dreams remain dreams because people are timid about risking in life.

Some people believe that structuring life to avoid as many risks as possible is the most sensible kind of life. I do not agree. One is certainly wise to avoid poor risks, or risks with long odds. But dreams will never become reality without some venturing and risking somewhere in life.

A teen-age girl came to see me about her problem with boys. She had dated a boy for several months and cared a great deal for him. Without warning, he had dropped her and treated her rather rudely. Since that time, she found it impossible to trust any of the boys that asked to date her or tried to be friends with her. She was able to admit to me that she could not trust people since she had gotten hurt.

"Sometimes people do get hurt when they trust other people," I said to her. "Risking is a part of loving. You always lay yourself open to hurt when you trust someone else. That is just the nature of loving. Some people can build a thick shell about themselves to keep from being hurt by people, but that is a terribly poor way to live."

If you love a number of people during your life, you will probably have to cope with someone's hurting you somewhere along the way. That young girl needed to learn that the thrill of loving is partly contained in having your trust in someone else justified. Loving always involves risking. Almost everything worth living for involves risking in some way.

Didn't God have to risk a lot when He offered His Son as an act of love for man? God loves; He risked because He loved that much; and then men killed the Son God offered.

It tells us something important about who God is, that He did not react to Jesus' death by building a shell around Himself, or by retaliating in anger. God might have been justified in saying to mankind: "I risked my own Son for you, and you rejected Him. Now I will punish you as you deserve to be punished."

He might have, but He did not. Instead, God took that potential tragedy and turned it into His greatest gift of all.

God is not afraid to risk. He sets the example we are to follow. God shares this earthly existence with us, in our terms. He has dealt with us through a Son, through love, and in grace. Those are all human terms and concepts.

Risk is one of the inevitable factors of life each man and woman will face. God helps us understand our relationship with Him by sharing in this human action—He

risks just like we risk. God does not require from us anything He is unwilling to share. In that way God sets the
example He wishes us to follow in life.

We understand how to react to risk by looking at God's
example. God could remain immovable and secure in His
infinite role as ruler of the universe. Instead He moves in
our world in terms we can understand and thereby shows
us the way to follow. God, by His very actions, is telling
you that risking is a necessary and rewarding part of living.

A young woman had real problems socializing with
other people her age because she felt inferior to most
other people. She came for some guidance about her problem and explained that this was very important to her.
She wanted more than anything to be more at ease at
parties and with other people her age. After a good deal
of conversation, it developed that she was making almost
no progress with her problem because she was terribly
afraid of risking in social situations. She was afraid that
if she spoke up and joined in, someone would criticize her,
or look down on her as an inferior person trying to butt
in. Risking ties in with self-image in many situations like
this one. A self-conscious person will be overly sensitive
to remarks or criticism. They will feel much more inadequate than they are seen by others.

Living takes courage, but it is worth every risk, every
venture into the unsure.

You can better understand attitudes toward death when
you learn to let go and live the great adventure of life.
Then you will know why those who have led the fullest of
lives are least afraid of death. Perhaps death looms most
unwelcomely to those who have not experienced the real
fullness of living.

One man's attitude toward death, which he told me one day with a great chuckle, may offer an insight into the inner confidence of one who knows life as a friend: "I'm not at all afraid of dying," he said, "but I sure will hate to stop living."

11 God's Power Can Change Your Life

The five principles of Power-Faith outlined so far might seem adequate for mastering life. In fact, they are not. There are six principles, and it is necessary for you to build a faith around all six. Principle six gives meaning to all the other five.

The sixth principle is this: *God is designed into His plan for life, and is the greatest source of power you have!*

Imagine the infinite power of God. With that awesome power the planets and stars were created. The earth was formed and man was brought forth upon it. Everything that is, has sprung from the mind of God as a part of His plan for life.

The New Testament is often called the Christian Gospel. *Gospel* is a Greek word which means *good news.* There is a recent translation of the New Testament, published by the American Bible Society, which is called Good News for Modern Man. What an exciting way to say it. The New Testament is Christ's good news about

111

God's love for man. This final principle of Power-Faith is part of that good news, too.

Principle six suggests two important facts about life. Both of these facts are of the greatest importance because they lay the basic foundation for understanding life. If either of the two were not true it would alter the whole meaning of life.

The first part of principle six says that God is a part of your life. There is no fact of life which would cause such profound change in the nature of things as God's absence would. God is present in your life because He wants to be. He has specifically designed Himself into His plan for life. God wants to be included in the affairs of the world.

There are many people who try to manage life with some variation or combination of the first five principles we have discussed. People keep trying to find an answer to successful living which does not require God's presence or participation. Each of us would like to believe it is our own talent and brilliance which accounts for our success in life. "The self-made man" is a favorite mental picture successful people have of themselves. The truth is, there are no self-made men. Every resource man works with is a gift of God, and has already been arranged into God's design for life.

It is useless to seek a life without God because God is a part of all life. The less you include God in your faith about life, the narrower your understanding of life will be.

Jesus spent much of his ministry talking to people about God's involvement with man. Over and over he talked about the Father's love for His children. He pictured God as one who pays very loving attention to all of His people.

How carefully the design of life was worked out.

Through the laws which govern the universe, God set in motion principles which man can count on. There was purpose in the plan for life. The Christian faith is a view which gives meaning to the plan. There is more to life than the physical laws, and God is present in the world to lend understanding to it all. God has a very definite purpose in mind for your living. He has not created you just to exist physically for a span of years. God has given you the opportunity to exist for a reason.

The New Testament does not mince words about the meaning of life. When Jesus was in Capernaum, a crowd of people found him by the sea and put to him some questions about his role in the world.

In response, Jesus spoke of himself as "the bread of life" and explained: "It is the spirit that gives life, the flesh is of no avail" (John 6:63).

All through the New Testament, the writers talk of God's giving new life to man. The important lesson about living which is found in the New Testament is that life means much more than physical existence. Life comes as a result of the way you have used your talents and opportunities. An existence which leaves God out is, at best, only a half-life, and can even be no life. It is quite possible for you to exist but be dead to real life.

The life spoken of in the Bible means an existence with real meaning. The first five principles of Power-Faith are means to that end. They are not the end product themselves. Many unhappy people think they can find ample fulfillment in life without God. They are convinced that all they need is to stumble onto the right situation or opportunity. They practice some version of the first five principles of Power-Faith, and then grow bitter in their

old age because they did not find the happiness of fulfillment they yearned for so long. Increasing self-esteem and
learning to manage life successfully are certainly necessary
to happiness and inner peace. They are only the beginning steps, though. They deal with the *how* of living, but
cannot begin to explain *why*, or for what end.

You need to ask yourself the question: "What do I do
with my life once I have learned how to manage it successfully?"

It is often true that you cannot move on to seek God's
will for you until you have made peace with yourself and
learned to function successfully in life. A frightened, limited person will be timid and unhappy. A person with poor
self-esteem and too little self-confidence will be living a
very incomplete existence. Only a person who feels himself to be someone of real worth, and who understands
how to make life work for his personal goals, will be able
to grow into a *whole* person.

The New Testament goes into considerable detail about
what makes someone a whole person. The complete person is one who is trying to be as much like God as possible. You are told in the Bible, very specifically, to imi-
tate God's attributes.

For that very reason, one of Jesus' most important roles
was to provide an example of how we should live. Jesus
was the most completely whole person who ever lived.

That merging of man with God is the key to becoming
a whole person. You are not whole all by yourself, no matter how well developed your talents are. You can be the
most self-confident person in the world and still be a very
incomplete person. It takes emotional health, confidence

in living, and spiritual openness to round out the complete person.

God has designed you so that you are incomplete without His own spirit to add the final dimension. It is impossible for a man to be complete all by himself. Only the man-God combination can form a complete person.

If you want to see what God's infinite power can do with a man's life, look to Jesus of Nazareth. There was in Him the ultimate blending of man and God.

Power-Faith is a process for becoming more of a whole person. In short, you are less than wholly developed as a person if you are functioning inadequately and using only a small portion of your potential. You are incomplete if you are unsuccessful at managing or coping with life. And just as importantly, you are less than whole if you fail to include God in your life.

You are not required by God to achieve perfection in life. You are required to strive for it, however. The command from God is to *seek* the kingdom of heaven.

In the earlier days of this country, there was a greeting in the Methodist tradition: "Brother, are you going on to perfection?" And the answer was: "The Lord willing, I am."

You won't be much use to yourself, or to anyone else, if you go through life feeling inferior and limited. Do not let worries about achieving perfection keep you from trying to grow. No matter how much you grow, emotionally or spiritually, you will never become perfect. You may become ten times the person you are now, but there will always be room for improvement. God does not hold that against you. You are not called to *be* perfect, but to *strive* for it. God expects you to attempt it with all your heart.

The secret God knows is that you will come closer than you would ever believe if you try with all your heart.

You have probably heard the old illustration about the church and the museum, because it has been around a long time, but it seems appropriate to mention it here: "The church is not a museum for saints, but a hospital for sinners."

If you are trying to find God's will for your life, a church can be of great help and comfort. You can find strength and support in the church. The struggles will be less lonely, and the rewards more meaningful if you can share them with others on the same path.

This sixth Power-Faith principle suggests a second important fact about life: God is not only present in your life, He is involved with it. God does more than merely exist in the world, He functions in life, also. God has designed for Himself an active role in existence.

The power of God can change your life if you will let Him work within you. You have known confident, successful people who refused to allow God in their lives. They are a completely different kind of person from one who uses his talents and potential in response to God's will.

You can develop more power for living than you are able to imagine, because you possess a remarkable depth of talent and potential. You will never achieve the wholeness needed to cope with every contingent of life, however, if you refuse to let the power of God work in you.

God is not present as an observer in life. He moves and acts positively to influence the order of things.

In the ages past, some religions taught that God created

the world, then sat back to watch in detached idleness. Other religions believed God pulled all the strings in life. They thought that every act, every happening, was due to God's manipulation.

The New Testament draws a line somewhere between those two views. God has established the laws of life to function continually. Basically, life moves under its own power, governed by the laws and properties built into existence. That is the basis of God's plan.

Even though He has created physical, biological, and mathematical laws to order life, God maintains His presence in the world as well. Out of God's love for you, He offers His personal warmth and comfort to make the universal laws less cold and relentless. The Holy Spirit moving in the world lends a more personal touch to life. In God's spirit there is care, and concern, and individual attention. It helps counteract the impersonality of natural law.

The law of gravity works the same day after day, no matter who is involved. Rain continues to fall on the just and the unjust. The seasons change, the earth turns, the tide moves in and out.

You cannot change the law of gravity, or hold back the tides. You *can* count, with certainty, on God's awareness of you, and of individual attention from Him. God is present in His handiwork. His presence and power in your life serve to complete you. They compliment the powers and abilities of your humanness.

The complete person is one who is open to God's movement and influence in his life. When you add the spiritual dimension to your life, it elevates you above mere humanness. You become an open being which extends on past human limits into the infinite spirit of God Himself.

In summary: It takes spiritual wholeness to round out physical and mental wholeness. Spiritual wholeness gives meaning and direction to emotional health, and successful management of life.

12 God Has Designed Life To Answer Prayer

Several important implications can be drawn from this sixth Power-Faith principle. One of the most crucial has to do with the way God answers prayer.

If God is present in the world and plays an active role in the affairs of man, it stands to reason that God reacts to the needs men have. We share our thoughts and needs with God by praying. What happens when we pray?

Some people believe prayer is a waste of time because God already knows everything and will be aware of our needs before we speak them. Others believe prayer is a waste of time because God does not act to intervene in life for any reason.

There are some who believe prayer is of great value just because it is a psychological exercise. They feel that while prayer is not actually heard by anyone, it is a good outlet for fears and frustrations. That school of thought suggests that prayer is good therapy because it allows the person to say the things which are weighing heavily upon him.

I believe God does hear prayer. It is the only belief which is consistent with an understanding of God actively and purposely designed into the structure of life. God not only hears prayer; He acts in response to prayer. God does answer prayer.

The six Power-Faith principles suggest a design for life which has an important implication for prayer: God has designed life to answer many prayers. The plan of life is God's loving, careful design. Why would He not use such an intricate and beautiful structure as a major tool to answer prayer? I believe God does use life to answer prayer.

People whose Christain faith is an escape from reality do not impress me. There are those who will tell you that science is religion's enemy. They live their lives as though religion is a fairy-tale world completely apart from real life. They separate religion from the world, and religiousness from participation in the fullness of living.

That is nonsense. Everything about Power-Faith thinking suggests that full, successful participation in life is the very plan God has for men. Religion is not intended as an escape for the weak. It is not a fairy tale for the comfort of those who are frightened by the prospect of facing reality. Sometimes I think people who wrap themselves in shallow religion are desperately hunting for an alternative to real life. That is false religion, because it tends to keep the weak from growing into strong persons.

The true Christian faith is a source of great strength. Real Christian faith is the source of infinite power through the development of your own potential, your ability to use life's resources and opportunities successfully, and your willingness to let God's power make you whole.

Life, in the Power-Faith view, is not your enemy, nor God's nemesis. Life is good. People can make life bad, but life is basically good. Life is God's loving creation and His greatest gift for you. Even Jesus is a part of the gift of life. Jesus was God's personal participation in the human drama of living on earth. Jesus' life is God's statement of the power possessed by a man perfectly attuned to God's will. There was nothing weak about Jesus. He was not limited in developing his own potential, and He was certainly not afraid to tackle life. His life, death, and Resurrection are a triumphal statement of God functioning perfectly through a human man.

The Christian faith offers hope and promise for the frightened and insecure. But it does not offer it through escape. Real faith offers the strength and power to develop the tremendous potential God has given you. It gives you the courage to approach life confidently, to see life as endless opportunity, and to use opportunity creatively and successfully. It offers all this in a framework of loving support and concern from God.

With this view of life, one grows through faith rather than escaping. Life is the gift of opportunity, not an enemy. Faith provides the power to develop strength, and confidence, and ability. A strong person who can manage life effectively will be quite an asset to God's work in the world.

God has provided life as the answer to many prayers if you will have faith that your answer can be found there. You cannot sit back and expect God to suddenly make everything different in your life. Many times you must provide the initiative and work to accomplish your prayer's fulfillment, but often the potential for answering your prayer has been provided already by God if you will be-lieve it is here. Ask God to give you the wisdom and in-sight to see the answer. He will certainly help you to find it.

Suppose someone has a serious drinking problem. Many prayers may be offered by loved ones who know the per-son and his problem. The prayers may not be answered right away. When you pray for others, there is always a chance that the person himself is blocking any help be-cause he does not want it. God has given man the freedom to make his own decisions in life. We are not robots. God respects that freedom and will not force Himself on a per-son's life if the person closes his heart to God.

If, finally, the person with a drinking problem reaches the point of wanting help himself and begins to pray along with those who have prayed for him, God can be-gin to act in his life. The ultimate answer to the drinking problem may be found in some of the gifts God has de-signed into life. Self-discipline and determination may be-gin the process. As the person frees himself from his de-pendence on alcohol and begins to function as a more adequate and normal person, his self-esteem may begin to rise. The long-term answer which can effectively change his behavior and personality might be the very factors of self-image and feelings of adequacy to cope with life, which we talked about in the early chapters of this book. Alcoholism is an escape from life. In this instance, prayers for someone with a drinking problem may well be an-swered through factors which have already been designed into life by God.

If prayers are for help in a time of loneliness, or for overcoming the emptiness left when a loved one is lost, the answers may already be present in life. God will help you find those answers. You will have to work with Him to make them effective, but there are many ways life can help you find answers to the problems you bear.

Giving yourself to help others may be an answer to your emptiness. Learning to feel at ease with other people may help brighten your loneliness. If the principles of life can give strength and happiness to you, are they not indeed a gift of God? Learning to develop your abilities and overcome your awe of life are ways God has of answering prayer.

Life may not answer all prayers. It can help with a great many prayers, though. Strength through faith opens unlimited horizons of possibility to you for utilizing God's magnificent gift of life.

13 Free To Soar the Heights

Once you were earthbound, tied to chains of inferiority and insecurity. Once you were imprisoned, walled behind invisible barriers invented in the mind. Once you limped painfully, struggling through life with a crippling self-image.

Now you are not chained. Your prison has melted away into the same recesses of your mind which spawned it. The barriers which limited your life have proven to be no barriers at all.

You know now that God can touch your life through His very loving care, and through the design of life He created because of His love for you.

Once you were pitifully incomplete and believed that person you were to be your destiny. Now you know the person you have been to be only a beginning of the person you will become.

Once you were not whole. Now you are whole, by God's infinite power, and through God's marvelous plan for life.

125

Now you know the truth about life. You know that you have barely begun to use the wellspring of potential within you. You know that life is designed in your favor. You know that God's own spirit makes you whole.

Now Jesus' words ring with new meaning as they speak directly to you: "If you continue in my word, you are truly my disciples, and you will know the truth, and the truth will make you free" (John 8:31, 32).

You *are* free! You have the greatest freedom of all—the freedom to become.

For the first time in your life, you are free to become whole, free to believe in yourself, free to face life unafraid. You are free to soar the heights of confident, creative living. You are free to live, with all that word implies.

God has created you with more potential than you could ever use. He has designed life to be the material and opportunity for your creativity.

To assure that you can become the complete person He planned you to be, God offers Himself as the ultimate power to make you whole. You cannot become whole all by yourself, but God working through you, coupled with your faith, can work a miracle in you. Power-Faith living can change your life if you will believe it can.

Faith is the key to your freedom. Faith unlocks the door. Faith has power to move mountains, or the power to change a life.

No one is limited to an inadequate life. No one is predestined to be insecure or to feel inferior. You will quite literally be the person you believe yourself to be. If you believe you must face life alone, you will be alone. If you know that God is a part of you and shares every load with you, God has promised it will be so.

Of course, this places a great responsibility on you. If you have digested the steps of Power-Faith and continue to believe it is hopeless to dream of a better life, you either refuse to believe these things are true, or you have not found the courage to risk your security for a higher goal.

The mental attitude you can develop with the six Power-Faith principles is not intended as an end in itself. It is the power you need to begin living successfully and confidently.

Now you have some decisions to make. You have to decide whether you really want a new life. You have to decide whether you want it badly enough to reshape your self-image, to overcome your awe of life, and to allow God to become a partner in your life.

Becoming a new person takes time. It takes awhile to digest all the implications of the six principles. It requires some honest hard work as well. If you really want the new confidence, if you really want a more successful life, the rewards outstrip the effort so greatly that every sacrifice pales beside them.

Power-Faith equips you with the understanding, the vision, and the capability to be God's whole person. The rest is up to you.

Joe E. Lewis said it his way, and no one has said it better: "You only live once, but if you play your cards right, once is enough!"